Women in the Old Testament
Part One

Women in the Old Testament
Part One

Irene Nowell, OSB

with **Jaime L. Waters**

and Little Rock Scripture Study staff

LITURGICAL PRESS
Collegeville, Minnesota

littlerockscripture.org

Cover design by John Vineyard. Interior art by Ned Bustard. Photos and illustrations on pages 19, 23, 39, 57, 70, 74, 79, 96, and 98 courtesy of Getty Images.

 This symbol indicates material that was created by Little Rock Scripture Study to supplement the biblical text and commentary. Some of these inserts first appeared in the *Little Rock Catholic Study Bible*; others were created specifically for this book by Catherine Upchurch.

1   2   3   4   5   6   7   8   9

Library of Congress Cataloging-in-Publication Data

Names: Nowell, Irene, 1940– author. | Waters, Jaime L., author. | Little Rock Scripture Study Staff, author.
Title: Women in the Old Testament / Irene Nowell, OSB, Jaime L. Waters and Little Rock Scripture Study Staff.
Description: Collegeville, [Minnesota] : Liturgical Press, 2024. | Series: Little Rock scripture study | Summary: "Women in the Old Testament explores Israel's beginnings, Israel's captivity and freedom, and Israel's tribal period from the perspective of the earliest women of salvation history, such as Sarah, Deborah, Ruth, Judith, and Esther. Includes classic commentary by Irene Nowell, OSB and contemporary scholarship by Jaime Waters. Study and reflection questions, prayers, and access to online lectures also included"— Provided by publisher.
Identifiers: LCCN 2024002658 (print) | LCCN 2024002659 (ebook) | ISBN 9780814668375 (v. 1 ; trade paperback) | ISBN 9780814668405 (v. 2 ; trade paperback) | ISBN 9780814668399 (v. 1 ; ebook) | ISBN 9780814668429 (v. 2 ; ebook)
Subjects: LCSH: Women in the Bible. | Bible Ole Testament | BISAC: RELIGION / Biblical Commentary / Old Testament / Prophets | RELIGION / Christianity / Catholic
Classification: LCC BS575 .N64 2024 (print) | LCC BS575 (ebook) | DDC 221.9/22082—dc23/eng/20240321
LC record available at https://lccn.loc.gov/2024002658
LC ebook record available at https://lccn.loc.gov/2024002659

TABLE OF CONTENTS

Wrap-Up Lectures and Discussion Tips for Facilitators are available for each lesson at no charge. Find them online at LittleRockScripture.org/Lectures/WomenOTPartOne.

Welcome

The Bible is at the heart of what it means to be a Christian. It is the Spirit-inspired word of God for us. It reveals to us the God who created, redeemed, and guides us still. It speaks to us personally and as a church. It forms the basis of our public liturgical life and our private prayer lives. It urges us to live worthily and justly, to love tenderly and wholeheartedly, and to be a part of building God's kingdom here on earth.

Though it was written a long time ago, in the context of a very different culture, the Bible is no relic of the past. Catholic biblical scholarship is among the best in the world, and in our time and place, we have unprecedented access to it. By making use of solid scholarship, we can discover much about the ancient culture and religious practices that shaped those who wrote the various books of the Bible. With these insights, and by praying with the words of Scripture, we allow the words and images to shape us as disciples. By sharing our journey of faithful listening to God's word with others, we have the opportunity to be stretched in our understanding and to form communities of love and learning. Ultimately, studying and praying with God's word deepens our relationship with Christ.

Women in the Old Testament, Part One

The resource you hold in your hands is divided into five lessons. Each lesson involves personal prayer and study using this book and the experience of group prayer, discussion, and wrap-up lecture.

If you are using this resource in the context of a small group, we suggest that you meet five times, discussing one lesson per meeting. Allow about 90 minutes for the small group gathering. Small groups function best with eight to twelve people to ensure good group dynamics and to allow all to participate as they wish.

Some groups choose to have an initial gathering before their regular sessions begin. This allows an opportunity to meet one another, pass out books, and, if desired, view the optional intro lecture for this study available on the "Resources" page of the Little Rock Scripture Study website (littlerockscripture.org). Please note that there is only one intro lecture for two-part studies.

Every Bible study group is a little bit different. Some of our groups like to break each lesson up into two weeks of study so they are reading less each week and have more time to discuss the questions together at their weekly gatherings. If your group wishes to do this, simply agree how much of each lesson will be read each week, and only answer the questions that correspond to the material you read. Wrap-up lectures can then be viewed at the end of every other meeting rather than at the end of every meeting. Of course, this will mean that your study will last longer, and your group will meet more times.

WHAT MATERIALS WILL YOU USE?

The materials in this book include:

- Scripture passages to be studied, using the New American Bible Revised Edition as the translation.
- Commentary by Irene Nowell, with introduction, updates, and essays by Jaime L. Waters.
- Occasional inserts 🔥 highlighting elements of the Scripture passages being studied. Some of these appear also in the *Little Rock Catholic Study Bible* while others are supplied by staff writers.
- Questions for study, reflection, and discussion at the end of each lesson.
- Opening and closing prayers for each lesson, as well as other prayer forms available in the closing pages of the book.

In addition, there are wrap-up lectures available for each lesson. Your group may choose to purchase a DVD containing these lectures or make use of the video lectures available online at no charge. The link to these free lectures is: LittleRockScripture.org/Lectures/WomenOTPartOne. Of course, if your group has access to qualified speakers, you may choose to have live presentations.

Each person will need a current translation of the Bible. We recommend the *Little Rock Catholic Study Bible*, which makes use of the New American Bible Revised Edition. Other translations, such as the New Jerusalem Bible or the New Revised Standard Version Updated Edition, would also work well.

HOW WILL YOU USE THESE MATERIALS?

Prepare in advance

Using Lesson One as an example:

- Begin with a simple prayer like the one found on page 11.

- Read the assigned material for Lesson One (pages 12–26) so that you are prepared for the weekly small group session.

- Answer the questions, Exploring Lesson One, found at the end of the assigned reading, pages 27–29.

- Use the Closing Prayer on page 30 when you complete your study. This prayer may be used again when you meet with the group.

Meet with your small group

- After introductions and greetings, allow time for prayer (about 5 minutes) as you begin the group session. You may use the prayer on page 11 (also used by individuals in their preparation) or use a prayer of your choosing.

- Spend about 45–50 minutes discussing the responses to the questions that were prepared in advance. You may also develop your discussion further by responding to questions and interests that arise during the discussion and faith-sharing itself.

- Close the discussion and faith-sharing with prayer, about 5–10 minutes. You may use the Closing Prayer at the end of each lesson or one of your choosing at the end of the book. It is important to allow people to pray for personal and community needs and to give thanks for how God is moving in your lives.

- Listen to or view the wrap-up lecture associated with each lesson (10–15 minutes). You may watch the lecture online, use a DVD, or provide a live lecture by a qualified local speaker. View the lecture together at the end of the session or, if your group runs out of time, you may invite group members to watch the lecture on their own time after the discussion.

A note to individuals

- If you are using this resource for individual study, simply move at your own pace. Take as much time as you need to read, study, and pray with the material.

- If you would like to share this experience with others, consider inviting a friend or family member to join you for your next study. Even a small group of two or three provides an opportunity for fruitful dialog and faith-sharing!

Women in the Old Testament

Part One

LESSON ONE

Introduction and
Women of Israel's Beginnings

Begin your personal study and group discussion with a simple and sincere prayer such as:

Prayer

God of Salvation, in these stories of biblical women, may we discover in ourselves a fresh desire to know and love you. Continue to form us as a people of your own.

Read the Introduction and pages 14–26, Lesson One.

Respond to the questions on pages 27–29, Exploring Lesson One.

The Closing Prayer on page 30 is for your personal use and may be used at the end of group discussion.

INTRODUCTION

In the original publication of *Women in the Old Testament*, Irene Nowell, OSB, states that the goal of the book is to tell the stories of biblical women. By telling their stories, Nowell encourages readers to study Scripture and use it for theological reflection. Nowell accomplishes her goal through a careful reading of biblical texts, offering insightful summaries and interpretations that help readers know and appreciate women in the Old Testament. Nowell's work was an important step forward in feminist biblical criticism and Catholic biblical exegesis, and it remains an invaluable resource for exploring biblical women.

Nowell reads with attention to the diverse ways women are depicted in Scripture and the implications of what texts say—and don't say—about women. Moreover, Nowell's readings are informed and grounded in her Benedictine charism, especially her interests in continued learning and encountering God in Scripture. Also notable is that Nowell achieved her goal while producing an accessible and engaging text for a wide-ranging audience. Since its publication in 1997, *Women in the Old Testament* has been an important volume that continues to advance the study of biblical women, especially in Catholic contexts.

Features of this Edition

This revised and updated edition of *Women in the Old Testament* maintains the spirit, interests, and vast majority of Nowell's book. As the editor of this work, I have been attentive to Nowell's style, content, and organization, revising and updating only as needed while relying on my own background as a contemporary scholar of the Old Testament and my particular teaching and research interests in the areas of women in Scripture as well as feminist and womanist biblical criticism. Some of the book's original language and content have been edited, updated, or adjusted in light of recent biblical scholarship, which tends to be more cautious about dating texts and identifying sources. All revisions have been made with the sole purpose of providing the most accurate and instructive interpretations for readers today.

Our current revisions also include an updated biblical translation. Since *Women in the Old Testament* was originally published, the New American Bible (NAB) has been revised. All biblical citations have therefore been updated to the New American Bible Revised Edition (NABRE).

A significant change to this commentary is the addition of "Continuing the Conversation" sections at the end of each lesson. Here, I have offered supplementary details, new perspectives, and further discussion of biblical characters and themes. This new content is designed to enrich your reflection on women in the Old Testament, building on Nowell's interpretations and adding another voice to the ongoing conversation. It is my hope that these sections will spark conversation within your small groups and provide opportunities for you to add your own voices to contemporary conversations about women in Scripture, in society, and in our church.

Briefer essays entitled "More Women of the Old Testament" can also be found throughout the study. Here I've provided a bit of information about other notable women of the Old Testament that you may find interesting. In addition to these essays, you'll find other informative inserts, indicated by a flame symbol, that are excerpted from the *Little Rock Catholic Study Bible* or written specifically for this study by Catherine Upchurch. At the end of each lesson, questions will help you reflect on and discuss what you've learned, and prayers will help you pray with the biblical texts and with your group.

The Women You Will Study

The content of *Women in the Old Testament* has been divided into two books for this Little Rock Scripture Study edition: Part One (5 lessons) and Part Two (4 lessons). Part One highlights women in the early stages of Israel's development, and Part Two focuses primarily on women after the establishment of the Israelite monarchy.

Part One of our study focuses on women who are found in the biblical books of Genesis through Ruth. Lessons One and Two center on women in Genesis. In Lesson One, Sarah and Hagar are highlighted, exploring the complex dynamics between these women, their roles as wives and mothers, and their relationships with Abraham. Lesson Two features additional women in the period of the matriarchs and patriarchs who are connected to Jacob: Rebekah (the wife of Isaac; Jacob's mother); Leah, Rachel, Bilhah, and Zilpah (Jacob's wives and their servants); Dinah (Jacob's daughter); and Tamar (the daughter-in-law of Jacob's son Judah). Lesson Three shifts to the book of Exodus, discussing the multiple women who helped to save Moses' life and make the exodus possible. In Lesson Four, women in the books of Joshua and Judges are explored. Some of these women are named, but there are several unnamed women in this lesson who are especially noteworthy. Lesson Five focuses on women in the book of Ruth and the beginning of 1 Samuel.

Each lesson examines a group of women, unpacking the main elements of their stories and, when relevant, considering how they interact with other women in the texts. The ways that women interact with, affect, or are affected by men in these narratives are also a significant aspect of our study. In exploring women who are important figures in the pre-monarchical narratives of ancient Israel, these lessons show the complexities and struggles that life in antiquity might have entailed. They also highlight the important roles women played in their families, communities, and in salvation history. Finally, our commentary provides opportunities to reflect on the actions of these women, the presence of God in their stories, and the ways biblical women might inspire faith and theological reflection in our lives today.

It is my hope that the structure and content of *Women in the Old Testament, Part One* and *Part Two* will provide an intellectually and spiritually stimulating approach to Bible study. As you embark on this journey, I invite you to enter with an open heart and mind as you encounter God through women in the Old Testament.

—Jaime L. Waters

Stories are a gift to the imagination. They help us imagine people, places, and experiences different from our own. They help us imagine the realities of our own lives in different terms. Biblical stories also help us imagine the relationship of God with human beings. They give us words to describe our own relationship with God.

It is only in recent years that attention has been given to the stories of biblical women. The growing awareness of women's stories has revealed a rich variety. There are stories of queens and slaves, assassins and victims of rape, mothers and wives, sisters and in-laws. Each of these women has unique characteristics. Each of these stories is food for our imaginations.

The Bible has also provided us with stories of what it means to be a woman created in the image of God and stories of God portrayed in the image of a woman.

This book tells the stories of only some of the women in the Old Testament. It is hoped that the introduction to their stories will encourage readers to search for more biblical women and also to find the story of faith reflected in the stories of their own lives.

—Irene Nowell, OSB

WOMEN OF ISRAEL'S BEGINNINGS

Scripture excerpts are found in shaded text boxes throughout the lesson. For additional context, you may wish to read all of the following in your Bible: Genesis 12; 15–17; 18:1-15; 21–23.

Our study begins with stories from the early era of Israel's patriarchs and matriarchs, beginning with Abraham and two women associated with his call, journey, and covenant: Sarah and Hagar. These stories from the book of Genesis explore the complexity of their paths and personalities while exposing challenges faced by women of their time.

SARAH

Sarah is the wife of Abraham. In Genesis 12–16, Sarah and Abraham are referred to as Sarai and Abram. In Genesis 17, the two receive new names to mark their covenantal relationship with God. Throughout this study, for consistency, we will refer to them as Sarah and Abraham. Sarah's first appearance is in the genealogy of Terah, Abraham's father (Gen 11:27-32). There we learn that she is the wife of Abraham, that she is barren, and that she has traveled with Terah and his family from Ur to Haran. These three elements—her husband, her barrenness, her traveling—will weave through Sarah's whole story.

The Journey

Genesis 12:4-5

[4]Abram went as the LORD directed him, and Lot went with him. Abram was seventy-five years old when he left Haran. [5]Abram took his wife Sarai, his brother's son Lot, all the possessions that they had accumulated, and the persons they had acquired in Haran, and they set out for the land of Canaan.

Abraham is called by God to leave his home and family and go to a new land. God promises that he will be blessed and that all nations will find blessing in him (Gen 12:1-3). Abraham obeys without a word, taking everything that belongs to him. Sarah is mentioned only as accompanying Abraham. We are reduced to speculation about her.

Abraham is seventy-five years old. By a process of deduction—Sarah is ten years younger than Abraham according to Genesis 17:17—we can assume that when she leaves Haran she is sixty-five. Two of the threads that weave through her story are already evident in these two verses. She is a faithful wife to Abraham, and she is again traveling. She, too, leaves home and family at the command of the God who speaks to Abraham. She believes in Abraham, who believes in God. She will be essential to God's fulfillment of the promises to Abraham, and through Abraham to all nations.

The rabbinic tradition speculates on what Sarah did for the ninety years while she was barren. It is said that she taught the other women about the one God. Because of the significance of her spiritual leadership, Abraham always set up her tent first (see Endnotes on p. 108).[1] In a patriarchal society it is rare to find such primary consideration given to women.

The tradition highlights the unique importance of Sarah, to whom even the great father Abraham defers.

Wife-Sister Stories

Genesis 12:10-20

[10]There was famine in the land; so Abram went down to Egypt to sojourn there, since the famine in the land was severe. [11]When he was about to enter Egypt, he said to his wife Sarai: "I know that you are a beautiful woman. [12]When the Egyptians see you, they will say, 'She is his wife'; then they will kill me, but let you live. [13]Please say, therefore, that you are my sister, so that I may fare well on your account and my life may be spared for your sake." [14]When Abram arrived in Egypt, the Egyptians saw that the woman was very beautiful. [15]When Pharaoh's officials saw her they praised her to Pharaoh, and the woman was taken into Pharaoh's house. [16]Abram fared well on her account, and he acquired sheep, oxen, male and female servants, male and female donkeys, and camels.

[17]But the Lord struck Pharaoh and his household with severe plagues because of Sarai, Abram's wife. [18]Then Pharaoh summoned Abram and said to him: "How could you do this to me! Why did you not tell me she was your wife? [19]Why did you say, 'She is my sister,' so that I took her for my wife? Now, here is your wife. Take her and leave!" [20]Then Pharaoh gave his men orders concerning Abram, and they sent him away, with his wife and all that belonged to him.

Abraham does not remain long in Canaan. Because of a famine in the land he moves on to Egypt. The basic plot of the wife-sister story appears three times (Gen 12:10-20; 20:1-18; 26:6-11). In each story the patriarch, either Abraham or his son Isaac, is afraid that someone will kill him in order to marry his beautiful wife. Therefore he tells the ruler of the land that his wife is his sister.

Two of these three stories are about Abraham and Sarah. In Genesis 12 we learn first of all that Sarah is beautiful. Abraham's perception of her is confirmed by the Egyptians. Pharaoh's courtiers praise Sarah to Pharaoh.

Sarah holds life and death. Abraham is afraid that he will be killed because of her. So Abraham wants her to claim to be his sister so that he "may fare well on [her] account and [his] life be spared for [her] sake." Abraham is right. Not only is his life spared; it goes very well with him and he is made wealthy because of her. Pharaoh's life is also in Sarah's hands. Because she is endangered, all living things in Pharaoh's house are threatened. He and his household are struck with severe plagues. When she is returned to Abraham, the plagues depart from Pharaoh's house. His plight foreshadows that of a later pharaoh who will be struck with plagues so that Sarah's descendants might be delivered from slavery (Exod 7:14–12:30).

The other wife-sister story (Gen 20:1-18) is similar. The king is Abimelech of Gerar. He discovers that Sarah is Abraham's wife through a dream in which God comes to him and says, "You are about to die because of the woman you have taken, for she has a husband" (20:3). Death and life are again in her hands.

 In Genesis, there are three versions of the **"wife-sister story"** in which a patriarch claims that his wife is really his sister in order to gain some benefit:

Genesis	Ancestors	Foreign Ruler	Means of Discovery
12:10-20	Abram and Sarai	Pharaoh in Egypt	Plagues
20:1-18	Abraham and Sarah	Abimelech of Gerar	Dream
26:6-11	Isaac and Rebekah	Abimelech of Gerar	Sees Isaac caressing Rebekah

Abimelech is threatened with death and told to "return the man's wife" so that his life might be spared. When Abimelech summons Abraham, Abraham defends himself by claiming that he thought he would be killed because of Sarah.

In this second story, God defends Sarah even when Abraham does not. "[T]he LORD had closed every womb in Abimelech's household on account of Abraham's wife Sarah" (20:18). Sarah, the barren woman, brings barrenness to Abimelech's household. When she is restored to her husband, God restores health to Abimelech's "wife, and his maidservants, so that they bore children" (20:17).

Not only is God concerned about Sarah's honor—so too is Abimelech. After he gave gifts to Abraham, he said to Sarah, "I hereby give your brother a thousand shekels of silver. This will preserve your honor before all who are with you and will exonerate you before everyone" (20:16).

In spite of Abraham apparently disowning her, Sarah is identified throughout both stories as his wife. She is called Abraham's wife six times in each story (12:11, 12, 17, 18, 19, 20; 20:2, 7, 11, 12, 14, 18). Sarah is restored to Abraham twice, but she remains barren, still waiting to bear his child. The two passages continue the story of her travels. She goes with Abraham to Egypt and to Gerar.

Descendants

Genesis 17:15-22

[15]God further said to Abraham: As for Sarai your wife, do not call her Sarai; her name will be Sarah. [16]I will bless her, and I will give you a son by her. Her also will I bless; she will give rise to nations, and rulers of peoples will issue from her. [17]Abraham fell face down and laughed as he said to himself, "Can a child be born to a man who is a hundred years old? Can Sarah give birth at ninety?" [18]So Abraham said to God, "If only Ishmael could live in your favor!" [19]God replied: Even so, your wife Sarah is to bear you a son, and you shall call him Isaac. It is with him that I will maintain my covenant as an everlasting covenant and with his descendants after him. [20]Now as for Ishmael, I will heed you: I hereby bless him. I will make him fertile and will multiply him exceedingly. He will become the father of twelve chieftains, and I will make of him a great nation. [21]But my covenant I will maintain with Isaac, whom Sarah shall bear to you by this time next year. [22]When he had finished speaking with Abraham, God departed from him.

More Women of the Old Testament

Lot's Wife and Daughters

Abraham has extended family through his nephew Lot, including Lot's wife and daughters. Genesis 19 tells the story of the destruction of the cities of Sodom and Gomorrah, and, in that context, Lot's wife loses her life and Lot's daughters are put in the vulnerable position of almost being offered by their father to a hostile mob. Lot's daughters then take advantage of their father to continue his family line by sexually assaulting him. The children of this assault are the Moabites and Ammonites, groups who are frequently enemies of Israel. The corrupt origins of these peoples are likely meant to disparage Israel's adversaries.

—*Jaime L. Waters*

The stories in Genesis 15–17 circle around the two poles of God's covenant promise to Abraham of descendants, and Sarah's continued childlessness. In Genesis 15, God promises Abraham descendants as many as the stars. Abraham has complained that, since he has no children, his servant Eliezer will be his heir. God reassures him, "[Y]our own offspring will be your heir" (15:4).

Sarah, however, is still barren and so she decides to give her servant Hagar to her husband Abraham so she might give him sons (16:1-6). In doing this she is following the Mesopotamian custom for a barren wife. The practice, which is described in law codes from Nuzi, was an ancient form of surrogate motherhood. The child born to the servant was to be considered the child of the wife. In the case of Sarah and Hagar this does not work. Sarah never claims Hagar's child. In fact, she eventually drives out both mother and child.

The incident with Hagar portrays the dark side of Sarah. After Hagar becomes pregnant, Sarah accuses Abraham of causing the conflict in the household. Abraham passes the responsibility back to Sarah, who abuses Hagar so much that she runs away. At the command of God's angel Hagar returns, only to be expelled again by her jealous mistress after the birth of Sarah's child. In her relationship with Hagar, Sarah appears cruel and ruthless.

In Genesis 17 God renews the covenant with Abraham and promises again that Abraham will be "the father of a multitude of nations" (17:4). Abraham thinks now that this promise will be fulfilled through Ishmael, Hagar's son (see 17:18). But God tells him that it is Sarah who will be the mother of the child of promise (17:16). Abraham's response is laughter. He cannot believe that he can beget a child at one hundred years of age or that Sarah can give birth at ninety (17:17). God, however, will not be stopped. God has and will protect Sarah throughout the wife-sister episodes and now reassures Abraham that the promise will come through Sarah. Not only Abraham is blessed in this chapter; not only Abraham has a formal naming, a sign of blessing (17:5-6). Sarah is blessed; Sarah is given a name (17:15-16). God promises, "I will bless her, and I will give you a son by her. Her also will I bless; she will give rise to nations, and rulers of peoples will issue from her" (17:16). Sarah is identified as the mother of the covenant and recipient of the covenant promises along with her husband Abraham.

 A **new name** often signifies an important change in someone's life. At critical moments, Abram's name is changed to Abraham, Sarai's to Sarah, and Jacob's to Israel (Gen 17:5, 15-16; 32:29). In these instances, their new names reflect God's intervention and promise in their lives.

Announcement of Birth

Genesis 18:1-15

[1]The LORD appeared to Abraham by the oak of Mamre, as he sat in the entrance of his tent, while the day was growing hot. [2]Looking up, he saw three men standing near him. When he saw them, he ran from the entrance of the tent to greet them; and bowing to the ground, [3]he said: "Sir, if it please you, do not go on past your servant. [4]Let some water be brought, that you may bathe your feet, and then rest under the tree. [5]Now that you have come to your servant, let me bring you a little food, that you may refresh yourselves; and afterward you may go on your way." "Very well," they replied, "do as you have said."

[6]Abraham hurried into the tent to Sarah and said, "Quick, three measures of bran flour! Knead it and make bread." [7]He ran to the herd, picked out a tender, choice calf, and gave it to a servant, who quickly prepared it. [8]Then he got some curds and milk, as well as the calf that had been prepared, and set these before them, waiting on them under the tree while they ate.

continue

> 9"Where is your wife Sarah?" they asked him. "There in the tent," he replied. 10One of them said, "I will return to you about this time next year, and Sarah will then have a son." Sarah was listening at the entrance of the tent, just behind him. 11Now Abraham and Sarah were old, advanced in years, and Sarah had stopped having her menstrual periods. 12So Sarah laughed to herself and said, "Now that I am worn out and my husband is old, am I still to have sexual pleasure?" 13But the LORD said to Abraham: "Why did Sarah laugh and say, 'Will I really bear a child, old as I am?' 14Is anything too marvelous for the LORD to do? At the appointed time, about this time next year, I will return to you, and Sarah will have a son." 15Sarah lied, saying, "I did not laugh," because she was afraid. But he said, "Yes, you did."

Three visitors come to Abraham and Sarah. After Abraham takes care of the needs of hospitality and they are fed with Sarah's help, one of them asks: "Where is your wife Sarah?" "There in the tent," Abraham replies. It seems that when male guests were being entertained, it was proper for the female members of the family to remain out of sight. Sarah, however, is not out of earshot. She is at the door of the tent, listening to the whole conversation.

The guest continues, "I will return to you about this time next year, and Sarah will then have a son." In this version of the story it is Sarah who laughs, well aware that she is no longer able to conceive. The visitor, however, also seems capable of hearing the conversation on both sides of the tent flap. He says, "Why did Sarah laugh? . . . Is anything too marvelous for the LORD to do?" The promise is renewed once more: Sarah will have a son. Sarah is afraid of this stranger who knows so much. She lies, saying, "I did not laugh." The stranger, however, is not deceived. "Yes, you did!"

By this time in the story attention has shifted from three visitors to one visitor, and that visitor has been identified as God (18:13). This story is yet another renewal of God's covenant promise that Abraham will have descendants, that they will be his own children, and that they will be the children of Sarah. The birth announcements in Genesis 17 and 18 take the following customary form:

1. Appearance of the Lord or an angel of the Lord (17:1; 18:1).
2. Expression of fear or reverence by the human being (17:3; 18:2).
3. The message (17:16; 18:10):
   a. A woman is pregnant and will bear a son.
   b. The son's name shall be . . .
   c. The future of the child will be . . .
4. Objection by the human being (17:17-18; 18:12).
5. Reassurance by God or the angel (17:19-21; 18:13-14).
6. The gift of a sign.

There are two stories of the announcement of Isaac's birth (Genesis 17 and 18) because the story was preserved in two traditions. The final editors of the Pentateuch (Genesis through Deuteronomy) kept multiple written traditions, even if stories repeated or contradicted each other.[2] In the two stories, there are two important omissions from the typical form. First of all, the child's name is given only in the reassurance. His name will be Isaac (*yishaq*), which means "he laughs." The name is suggested in both announcement stories. The objection in both stories is laughter: Abraham laughs in 17:17; Sarah laughs in 18:12. Secondly, there is no sign given in either story. In Genesis 17, circumcision is given as a sign of the covenant; in Genesis 18, the extraordinary knowledge of the visitor might be construed as a sign. Or perhaps the child himself is to be seen as a sign, not only of the truth of the announcement story but also of God's fidelity to the covenant promise.

Both announcement stories reveal that Sarah, as well as Abraham, is chosen by God. She is the mother of the promise. Sarah is capable and still works hard at the tasks of hospitality even when she is ninety years old. Sarah has a lively sense of humor and a strong dose of reality. She also knows fear and succumbs to deceit when the stranger quizzes her concerning her laughter. She is a strong woman and a complex character.

Sarah and Her Son

Genesis 21:1-8

¹The LORD took note of Sarah as he had said he would; the LORD did for her as he had promised. ²Sarah became pregnant and bore Abraham a son in his old age, at the set time that God had stated. ³Abraham gave the name Isaac to this son of his whom Sarah bore him. ⁴When his son Isaac was eight days old, Abraham circumcised him, as God had commanded. ⁵Abraham was a hundred years old when his son Isaac was born to him. ⁶Sarah then said, "God has given me cause to laugh, and all who hear of it will laugh with me. ⁷Who would ever have told Abraham," she added, "that Sarah would nurse children! Yet I have borne him a son in his old age." ⁸The child grew and was weaned, and Abraham held a great banquet on the day of the child's weaning.

demands of Abraham: "Drive out that slave and her son" (Gen 21:10). God tells a distressed Abraham, "Obey Sarah, no matter what she asks of you; for it is through Isaac that descendants will bear your name" (Gen 21:12). God is still taking note of Sarah, even though it seems that her importance is overshadowed by that of her son. Abraham, the father of God's covenant people, is instructed to obey his wife.

Sarah, who seems overly protective of Isaac in the story of Ishmael, is absent from the story of Abraham's near sacrifice of her son (Gen 22:1-19). We are reduced again to speculation. Is it Sarah who must let go of this son to whom she is so fiercely attached? Did Abraham tell Sarah his purpose when the two left for Mount Moriah? What did Isaac say to his mother when they returned?

It seems strangely significant that the next mention we have of Sarah is the report of her death (Gen 23:1-2). The span of her life was 127 years; we are told she lived almost 40 years after the birth of Isaac. Abraham mourns for her according to custom and then sets out to find a place for her burial. He buys the cave of Machpelah near Hebron from the Hittites and buries her there. When he dies he is buried

"The LORD took note of Sarah as . . . promised. Sarah became pregnant and bore Abraham a son" (21:1-2). Sarah is specifically named as the one who receives the promise. Sarah, who states that God kept her from bearing children (Gen 16:2), now recognizes that it is through God that her child is born. Her response bears witness again to her sense of humor and her ability to laugh at herself. Now she says, "God has given me cause to laugh." Sarah also knows her own part in this happy event. "I have borne [Abraham] a son in his old age." God and Sarah have given Abraham a son, the child of promise.

Sarah's struggles are not over, however. Sarah notices Ishmael, Hagar's son, playing with Isaac, and

Sarah laughs as visitors tell Abraham she will bear a son. Julius Schnorr von Carolsfeld (1860).

there with her (Gen 25:9-10) and eventually Isaac and Rebekah, Jacob and Leah will also be buried there. The burial cave is the only land ever owned by Abraham, this man who was promised land, descendants, and a special relationship with God. Sarah is significant in the fulfillment of all God's promises to Abraham.

The final note about Sarah returns to the important relationship between mother and son. Isaac takes his new wife into the tent of his mother Sarah and, in his love for Rebekah, finds comfort after Sarah's death (Gen 24:67).

Who is Sarah?

Sarah is wife to Abraham, sharing in all his travels, his trials, and God's covenant promises to him. After ninety years of barrenness, she becomes the mother of Isaac, the covenant child. She begins a long line of barren women who mother children of promise: Rebekah, Rachel, Hannah (mother of Samuel), and Elizabeth (mother of John the Baptist). The line comes to its ultimate fullness in a woman who, although remaining a virgin, also becomes a mother. Through the power of God's spirit, Mary gives birth to the child who is hope for all of us. Is anything impossible for God? Like Mary, Sarah is also a model of the church who mothers the people of God. Paul tells Christians: "You . . . are children of the promise . . . children not of the slave woman [Hagar] but of the freeborn woman [Sarah]" (Gal 4:28, 31).

HAGAR

Maid of Sarah

Genesis 16:1-6

[1]Abram's wife Sarai had borne him no children. Now she had an Egyptian maidservant named Hagar. [2]Sarai said to Abram: "The LORD has kept me from bearing children. Have intercourse with my maid; perhaps I will have sons through her." Abram obeyed Sarai. [3]Thus, after Abram had lived ten years in the land of Canaan, his wife Sarai took her maid, Hagar the Egyptian, and gave her to her husband Abram to be his wife. [4]He had intercourse with her, and she became pregnant. As soon as Hagar knew she was pregnant, her mistress lost stature in her eyes. [5]So Sarai said to Abram: "This outrage against me is your fault. I myself gave my maid to your embrace; but ever since she knew she was pregnant, I have lost stature in her eyes. May the LORD decide between you and me!" [6]Abram told Sarai: "Your maid is in your power. Do to her what you regard as right." Sarai then mistreated her so much that Hagar ran away from her.

Hagar is the "maid of Sarai" (Gen 16:8), an Egyptian (16:1). Is she one of "the persons" Abraham had acquired in Haran (Gen 12:5)? She appears first by name in Genesis 16 when Sarah decides to use her as a surrogate mother in order to give sons to Abraham. Sarah says, "I will have sons through her." Through the first three verses of this chapter Hagar is the object of others' actions: Sarah had a maid; Sarah gave Hagar to Abraham; he had intercourse with her. For a fleeting moment she becomes the subject: She became pregnant; she became aware of her pregnancy; she looked on her mistress with disdain. But Sarah does not allow Hagar to take her place for long. She complains to Abraham who says, "Your maid is in your power." Sarah then abuses Hagar so much that she runs away.

 Considering the overarching story of salvation history, there is a certain **irony** in the fact that Sarah's maid, a slave with no rights, is said to be an Egyptian (Gen 16:1). Within a few centuries, the descendants of Sarah and Abraham will be enslaved in Egypt (Exod 1:8-11). Throughout the ambiguities of history, God is present with all who call out in times of need.

The incident, however, has given Hagar a certain status. She is given to Abraham not as a concubine but "to be his wife" (16:3) As a second wife she has certain rights, particularly in consequence of her pregnancy.

The ancient law code of Hammurabi provides a context by which to understand Sarah's giving of her maid to her husband. There is precedent for a barren wife using a slave as a surrogate mother. Sarah's complaint against Hagar is also clarified by this law code. The slave who bears the master's children may not consider herself to have the same legal standing as the wife.[3] Even so, the wife may not sell the slave. But may she drive her out? Is Hagar still a slave, or is she a wife?

Vision in the Desert

Genesis 16:7-16

[7]The LORD's angel found her by a spring in the wilderness, the spring on the road to Shur, [8]and he asked, "Hagar, maid of Sarai, where have you come from and where are you going?" She answered, "I am running away from my mistress, Sarai." [9]But the LORD's angel told her: "Go back to your mistress and submit to her authority. [10]I will make your descendants so numerous," added the LORD's angel, "that they will be too many to count." [11]Then the LORD's angel said to her:
"You are now pregnant and shall bear a son;
  you shall name him Ishmael,
For the LORD has heeded your affliction.
[12]He shall be a wild ass of a man,
  his hand against everyone,
  and everyone's hand against him;
Alongside all his kindred
  shall he encamp."
[13]To the LORD who spoke to her she gave a name, saying, "You are God who sees me"; she meant, "Have I really seen God and remained alive after he saw me?" [14]That is why the well is called Beer-lahai-roi. It is between Kadesh and Bered.

[15]Hagar bore Abram a son, and Abram named the son whom Hagar bore him Ishmael. [16]Abram was eighty-six years old when Hagar bore him Ishmael.

The word "angel" means "messenger" in the biblical languages of Hebrew and Greek. In the Pentateuch (the first five books of the Bible) **angels** are often a sign of God's own presence. In fact, the biblical writers often interchange "angel" or "messenger" with "God" or "LORD" in the space of a single story, such as that found in Genesis 16:7-16 (see especially verses 7, 9, 11, 13).

The fleeing Hagar meets a messenger of God, an angel of the Lord. First the messenger asks her a powerful question: "Hagar, maid of Sarai, where have you come from and where are you going?" (16:8). She answers truthfully, "I am running away from my mistress, Sarai" (16:8). However, she has no answer concerning where she is going. The messenger gives the difficult answer to that question: "Go back to your mistress."

But the messenger has another message for Hagar. The central elements of the announcement of birth form (see above p. 18) are easily recognized:

1. The appearance of an angel of the Lord (16:7).

3. The message (16:11-12).

   a. Hagar is pregnant and will bear a son (16:11).

   b. The son's name shall be Ishmael, "God hears" (16:11).

   c. The future of the child will be strife (16:12).

The form is abbreviated. There is no expression of fear or reverence (#2), nor is there an objection

(#4). Therefore, there is no need for either reassurance (#5) or a sign (#6).

It should be noted, however, that this is the first time in the Bible that the birth announcement form appears. Hagar is the first person in the Bible to be visited by an angel. She is the first to hear an announcement of birth. She is the first woman to bear a child in the story of the ancestors (Gen 12–50). She is promised descendants by the same terms typically given to male ancestors (Gen 16:10; cf. Gen 15:5; 17:5-6; 22:16-17; 26:4; 28:14).

 Most covenants described in the Bible are attached to male figures, even when women are involved (e.g., God's covenant with Abraham involved Sarah as the mother of descendants but is only directly made with Abraham). Explicitly **naming women** would have seemed unnecessary in the ancient Mediterranean world where women were generally seen as the property of men. But we find an exception with Hagar, as God promises her that she will have numerous descendants (Gen 16:10), just as God promises Abraham (Gen 13:16).

Hagar is the only person in the Bible to give a name to God: "To the LORD who spoke to her she gave a name, saying, 'You are God who sees me'" (Gen 16:13). In all of Hagar's story, only God, whether in person or through a messenger, speaks to Hagar. Only God calls her by name. (Sarah and Abraham consistently refer to her as "maid" or "slave.") It is God who sees Hagar as a person, hears her, sends a messenger to her, names her, makes her mother of a nation. Hagar in turn sees God as a person and gives a name to God: *el-roi*, "the God who sees."

Hagar returns to the house of Abraham and bears him a son according to the angel's promise. Abraham (instead of Hagar) names this first-born son the name that the angel had given him, Ishmael, which is interpreted, "God hears." Abraham is eighty-six years old at the time of Ishmael's birth. We are not told Hagar's age.

Expulsion

Genesis 21:9-13

⁹Sarah noticed the son whom Hagar the Egyptian had borne to Abraham playing with her son Isaac; ¹⁰so she demanded of Abraham: "Drive out that slave and her son! No son of that slave is going to share the inheritance with my son Isaac!" ¹¹Abraham was greatly distressed because it concerned a son of his. ¹²But God said to Abraham: Do not be distressed about the boy or about your slave woman. Obey Sarah, no matter what she asks of you; for it is through Isaac that descendants will bear your name. ¹³As for the son of the slave woman, I will make a nation of him also, since he too is your offspring.

After the birth of Isaac (Gen 21:1-8), Sarah is intent that everything—wealth, attention, blessing—will go to her son. "No son of *that slave* is going to share the inheritance with my son Isaac" (21:10, emphasis mine). The sight of Ishmael playing with Isaac is enough cause for her to demand that Abraham once more expel Hagar along with her son. The Hebrew text simply says that she saw Ishmael "playing." The phrase "with her son Isaac" is missing from the original Hebrew text but is found in the Septuagint (Greek) and in the Vulgate (Latin). A pun may cast light on Sarah's difficulty. Ishmael's "play" is *mesaheq* in Hebrew, from the same root (*shq*) as Isaac's name. Ishmael is "Isaac-ing." In no way is Sarah going to allow Ishmael to take Isaac's place, even in "play."

Sarah demands that Abraham expel Hagar and Ishmael. Abraham is initially unwilling, "because it concerned a son of his." Hagar's value has diminished now that she has borne Abraham a son. God, however, has not forgotten her. "Do not be distressed about the boy *or about your slave woman*" (21:12, emphasis mine). But then even God's attention seems to move elsewhere. God reminds Abraham that it is Sarah who mothers the child of promise. As an afterthought, God promises nations to Ishmael because he is *Abraham's* offspring. Hagar has virtually disappeared.

There are some legal implications to this incident. The Deuteronomic law code states:

If a man has two wives, one loved and the other un-loved, and if both the loved and the unloved bear him sons, but the firstborn is the son of the unloved wife: when he comes to bequeath his property to his sons he may not consider as his firstborn the son of the wife he loves, in preference to the son of the wife he does not love, the firstborn. On the contrary, he shall recognize as his firstborn the son of the unloved wife, giving him a double share of whatever he happens to own, since he is the first fruits of his manhood, and to him belong the rights of the firstborn. (Deut 21:15-17)

The inheritance rights of the child of a slave are described in the code of Hammurabi, an older legal collection from ancient Mesopotamia:

If a citizen who has children by his wife and by his slave adopts the slave's children, his estate shall be divided evenly between the children of both, after his wife's firstborn son receives the preferential share.[4]

Hagar and Ishmael in the desert. Gustave Dore (1897).

Several questions arise regarding the status of Hagar and of her son Ishmael. Is Hagar Abraham's second wife as Genesis 16:3 implies? If so, the later Deuteronomic law code protects against abuses such as Abraham's against Hagar and Ishmael. Or is Hagar simply the slave who is a surrogate mother? Hammurabi's law would have required Abraham to grant Ishmael part of the inheritance, since he has certainly adopted him. Abraham names him (Gen 16:15), claims him (17:18), is concerned for him (21:11). Even in the ancient world the treatment of Hagar is against the law, as well as against human compassion.

Desert Revisited

Genesis 21:14-21

[14]Early the next morning Abraham got some bread and a skin of water and gave them to Hagar. Then, placing the child on her back, he sent her away. As she roamed aimlessly in the wilderness of Beer-sheba, [15]the water in the skin was used up. So she put the child down under one of the bushes, [16]and then went and sat down opposite him, about a bowshot away; for she said to herself, "I cannot watch the child die." As she sat opposite him, she wept aloud. [17]God heard the boy's voice, and God's angel called to Hagar from heaven: "What is the matter, Hagar? Do not fear; God has heard the boy's voice in this plight of his. [18]Get up, lift up the boy and hold him by the hand; for I will make of him a great nation." [19]Then God opened her eyes, and she saw a well of water. She went and filled the skin with water, and then let the boy drink.

[20]God was with the boy as he grew up. He lived in the wilderness and became an expert bowman. [21]He lived in the wilderness of Paran. His mother got a wife for him from the land of Egypt.

Hagar wanders again in the desert. The supplies provided by Abraham run out and both Hagar and her son face death. She places the child at a distance in order not to see him die. Then she begins to cry. The Hebrew tradition states that Hagar cried (21:16), but the Greek tradition says Ishmael cried. This may be an attempt to harmonize verse 16 with verse 17, which indicates it is the boy's voice that God hears. The angel of God returns and renews the promise that Ishmael will grow into a great nation. Then this woman of vision sees again: "God opened her eyes, and she saw a well of water" (21:19).

Hagar and her son remain in the desert. The story continues to focus on Ishmael. God is with him. His mother gets a wife for him from Egypt, her homeland. Ishmael lives to a ripe old age and becomes the father of twelve tribes (Gen 25:12-18). They are listed as enemies of the twelve tribes of Israel: "The tents of Edom and the Ishmaelites, / of Moab and the Hagrites" (Ps 83:7). They are without the wisdom that belongs to Israel: "The descendants of Hagar who seek knowledge on earth, / the merchants of Medan and Tema, / the storytellers and those seeking knowledge— / These have not known the way to wisdom, / nor have they kept her paths in mind" (Bar 3:23).

Who is Hagar?

In the beginning of the story Hagar is called *shiphah*, "maid" (Gen 16:1, 2, 3, 5, 6, 8; cf. 25:12). Sarah gives her to Abraham as a "wife," *ishshah* (Gen 16:3). When Sarah drives her out with Ishmael, both Sarah and God refer to Hagar as a "slave," *amah* (Gen 21:10, 12, 13).

The tension in the story may turn on the struggle between Hagar's roles. Is Hagar the surrogate mother, and is her son therefore to be considered the son of Sarah? Or is Hagar the wife who bears the firstborn to Abraham? Is Ishmael to be considered Abraham's firstborn son with the rights of the firstborn? Is he the son of a slave woman, who does not have the rights of the firstborn, but does have a right

to inherit? This tension may explain Hagar's disdainful attitude toward Sarah and Sarah's abuse of Hagar (Gen 16:6). It may also explain Sarah's fear that Ishmael will inherit along with Isaac (Gen 21:10). Hagar's status may have improved with her pregnancy and childbearing, but her situation certainly did not.

Nonetheless, Hagar is a significant person in the ancestor story. She is intimately involved with the covenant promise to Abraham of descendants. She is a woman of vision. She sees and names God; she sees God's gifts and providence. Although Hagar is not part of the ongoing history of God's covenant people, the stories concerning her seem to be told from her viewpoint. Though seemingly powerless as female, slave, and foreigner, Hagar becomes the mother of a nation.

And yet Hagar remains an outcast. In Christian tradition, she (the foreign woman) ironically becomes the symbol of Judaism, the old covenant, and Sarah (the mother of the Jewish people) becomes the symbol of Christianity. Paul writes to the Galatians: "Now this is an allegory. These women represent two covenants. One was from Mount Sinai, bearing children for slavery; this is Hagar. Hagar represents Sinai, a mountain in Arabia; it corresponds to the present Jerusalem, for she is in slavery along with her children" (Gal 4:24-25). In this allegory Paul is using strong language to contrast Judaism with Christianity. He describes Judaism as if it were enslaved to an over-literal interpretation of the law and Christianity as set free by Christ. His point is that the true law for both Jews and Christians is the law of love: "In Christ Jesus, neither circumcision nor uncircumcision counts for anything, but only faith working through love" (Gal 5:6). Hagar suffers yet again in comparison to Sarah. She is the symbol of slavery, Sarah, the symbol of freedom. Yet it is only in the reconciliation of their children that all the descendants of Abraham will be able to rejoice in God's kingdom.

CONTINUING THE CONVERSATION

By Jaime L. Waters

Hagar: Oppressed and Empowered

Inspiration for the Oppressed

In Genesis 16 and 21, the interactions between Hagar, Sarah, and Abraham are filled with problematic power dynamics that lead to Hagar's physical, sexual, mental, and emotional abuse. As a woman who is an Egyptian slave, Hagar has been an inspirational biblical figure, especially for people who are oppressed and disenfranchised, in particular African American women.

In her work *Sisters in the Wilderness: The Challenge of Womanist God-Talk*, Delores S. Williams highlights Hagar's struggles in Genesis and puts them in conversation with the struggles of African American women. Williams notes how issues of sexual violence, coerced surrogacy, economic disparities, and homelessness resonate with the historical oppressions of African American women. Williams also highlights the hope and resilience that Hagar and African American women demonstrate, especially when calling out to God in the midst of struggles.

A Figure of Empowerment

While systems of oppression should not be overlooked, Hagar should also be viewed as a figure of empowerment. In Genesis 16, Hagar's decision to leave her abusive situation is incredibly important. She shows power and agency by leaving, and when she is visited by an angel, she speaks for the first time in the narrative, confirming her powerful action: "I am running away from my mistress, Sarai" (16:8).

The angel's response presents challenges to readers, as the angel tells Hagar to return and submit. We can immediately identify a host of problems with this declaration, including its potential to be misused to suggest that people who have been abused should return to their abusers.

This type of reading must be avoided; instead, we should keep the larger literary context in mind. The Abraham story is focused on covenant, with a recurring promise of descendants. Hagar is needed as a part of Abraham's blessed progeny, so as a character in this narrative, she cannot leave the story just yet. Williams suggests that the angel's instruction for Hagar to return is for her own survival and the survival of her unborn son, Ishmael, an interpretation that may be supported by Genesis 16:10-12, which includes blessings for Ishmael. This reading could lessen some of the sting of the angel's instruction, but, given the difficulties and hostility that Hagar and Ishmael encounter when they return, the angel's command still poses significant theological challenges.

Hagar exits the story in Genesis 21, which is often framed as her banishment. Nowell's treatment on Hagar, for example, refers to this text as "Expulsion," but it might be better to think of her exit as her "Freedom." While Abraham does indeed push out Hagar and Ishmael (their son) so he can prioritize Sarah and Isaac, the result is that Hagar is finally away from abuse. This is not to suggest that Hagar's life of freedom will be easy. Indeed, the texts we have about Hagar attest to the challenges she faces as a single mother with limited resources. Yet framing her departure as freedom opens the possibility of seeing her life after slavery in a much more positive way.

Hagar in Islamic Tradition

Historically, Hagar has not held a significant role in Jewish and Christian tradition, although there are contemporary efforts to amplify her story and reclaim her as an important biblical woman who overcomes adversity and toward whom God shows special interest and care. In

Islamic tradition, Hagar (*Hajar* in Arabic) is a significant figure. She is honored as an important matriarch and wife of Abraham (*Ibrahim*). Some biblical traditions are alluded to in Islamic texts such as the Quran and *hadith* (sayings or traditions associated with Muhammad).

Some Islamic traditions record similar content to what is found in Genesis, though there are sometimes variances. For instance, in Genesis 21, Hagar and Ishmael run out of water after being sent away. Hagar cries out to God for help and is answered with verbal reassurance and the appearance of a well of water to sustain them. In Islamic tradition, Hajar's crying out occurs in Mecca, and she runs between two hills, Safa and Marwah, in search of water. Islamic tradition holds that Hajar ran between the hills seven times, and then a well (the Zamzam Well) appeared. To honor Hajar, during the Islamic pilgrimage (*hajj*), pilgrims run between the two hills to commemorate Hajar's prayerful action and God's faithful response during her time of need.

EXPLORING LESSON ONE

1. What brings you to this study of women in the Old Testament? Why do you think their stories still have significance in our time and culture?

_____

_____

_____

_____

_____

2. Only Abraham is directly called by God to journey to a new land, but his family accompanies him (Gen 12:1-6). According to the commentary, what is the rabbinic tradition about how Sarah lived at this time? How might this way of life have influenced what she understood as her own personal call?

_____

_____

_____

_____

_____

3. What is your reaction to the account of Abraham lying about Sarah's identity in order to protect himself and grow prosperous (Gen 12:13-16)? (See also 20:2, 11, 14-15.) How does Sarah's vulnerability relate to the situation of women in today's world? And what does God's protection of Sarah in these stories tell you about God's treatment of the vulnerable?

_____

_____

_____

_____

4. Sarah has a clear role in God's promise of descendants (Gen 17:15-21; 18:9-14), but she chooses to take matters into her own hands by offering Hagar to Abraham. Are there times in your own life that have convinced you that God is more than capable of the "impossible"? (See Gen 18:14; Matt 19:26; Mark 9:23.)

_____

_____

_____

_____

5. Sarah is depicted as laughing twice in these stories (Gen 18:12; 21:6). What are the unique occasions for her laughter, and how does her laughter change? What do these narrative details add to your understanding of Sarah's life and personality?

_____

_____

_____

_____

_____

_____

6. a) Early in the travel narrative of Abraham and Sarah, it is Sarah who is vulnerable and in need of protection. Later in the story, Sarah seems to have forgotten what it feels like to be vulnerable. What do you make of Sarah's treatment of Hagar, her maid (Gen 16:1-6; 21:9-13)?

_____

_____

_____

_____

_____

b) How does God see Hagar differently than Sarah sees Hagar (Gen 16:7-16)?

_____

_____

_____

_____

_____

7. In Genesis 16:13 Hagar gives a name to God: "God who sees me." What do you think it means to be seen by God, to be recognized and known by the divine? What does this say about human dignity?

_____

_____

_____

_____

_____

_____

8. How does St. Paul later symbolically use a reference to Sarah and Hagar? (See Gal 4:22-31.) Why is this ironic?

_____

_____

_____

_____

_____

_____

9. If you could speak with Sarah and/or Hagar, what would you want to know about their lives and experiences of God?

_____

_____

_____

_____

_____

_____

10. Continuing the Conversation (see pp. 25–26): Hagar and her experiences have been perceived in a variety of ways over time. In what way do you most relate to Hagar? How does her story trouble or inspire you?

_____

_____

_____

_____

_____

_____

CLOSING PRAYER

Prayer

"Why did Sarah laugh and say, 'Will I really bear a child, old as I am?' Is anything too marvelous for the LORD to do?"

(Gen 18:13-14)

God of Wonders, your vision for us is always more than we can imagine. Like Sarah and Hagar, we hesitate to believe in such generosity and mercy. Patiently lead us into the kind of faith that trusts in you, our Maker, faithful and true. We pray together for those who are searching for their life's purpose, especially . . .

LESSON TWO

More Women of Israel's Beginnings

Begin your personal study and group discussion with a simple and sincere prayer such as:

Prayer

> *God of Salvation, in these stories of biblical women, may we discover in ourselves a fresh desire to know and love you. Continue to form us as a people of your own.*

Read pages 32–49, Lesson Two.

Respond to the questions on pages 50–52, Exploring Lesson Two.

The Closing Prayer on page 52 is for your personal use and may be used at the end of group discussion.

MORE WOMEN OF ISRAEL'S BEGINNINGS

Scripture excerpts are found in shaded text boxes throughout the lesson. For additional context, you may wish to read all of the following in your Bible: Genesis 24; 25:19-34; 26:6-11; 27:1-46; 28:1-5; 29:1-35; 30:1-43; 31:14-35; 34; 35:16-20; 38.

As Israel's period of patriarchs and matriarchs continues, we turn to the descendants of Abraham and their wives, as well as women who are identified as their nurses or servants. Stories of faith, family, violence, and struggle continue to paint a complex portrait of the biblical women of their era.

REBEKAH

Betrothal

Rebekah is the daughter of Bethuel and granddaughter of Abraham's brother Nahor and his wife Milcah (Gen 22:23). She becomes the wife of Isaac, the son of Abraham and Sarah, the child of promise.

The story of Rebekah's betrothal to Isaac is one of the longest chapters in Scripture (Gen 24). The narrative is a type scene, a literary convention in which the narrator is expected to include a specific set of elements as the story is told. The set of expected elements for the betrothal type scene include: a stranger, a well, a young woman, haste, drawing water, and sharing a meal. All the expected elements are found in Genesis 24.

Abraham, interested in the continuation of God's promise through descendants, sends his servant back to Mesopotamia to find a wife for Isaac (24:1-9). When the servant expresses some fear, Abraham assures him, "[God] will send his angel before you, and you will get a wife for my son there."

Many stories of **betrothal** in the Old Testament contain the same key elements, as in these three examples:

	Isaac and Rebekah Gen 24:1-67	Jacob and Rachel Gen 29:1-30	Moses and Zipporah Exod 2:15-22
Arrival of stranger	24:10-14	29:1	2:15
Well	24:15-16	29:2	2:16
Young woman	24:11	29:6, 9	2:16
Drawing water	24:16-20	29:10	2:17
Haste	24:17-18, 20, 28, 30, 33, 55-56	29:10-13	----
Invitation to meal	24:33	----	2:20
Marriage	24:67	29:21-30	2:21

Genesis 24:10-14

¹⁰The servant then took ten of his master's camels, and bearing all kinds of gifts from his master, he made his way to the city of Nahor in Aram Naharaim. ¹¹Near evening, at the time when women go out to draw water, he made the camels kneel by the well outside the city. ¹²Then he said: "LORD, God of my master Abraham, let it turn out favorably for me today and thus deal graciously with my master Abraham. ¹³While I stand here at the spring and the daughters of the townspeople are coming out to draw water, ¹⁴if I say to a young woman, 'Please lower your jug, that I may drink,' and she answers, 'Drink, and I will water your camels, too,' then she is the one whom you have decided upon for your servant Isaac. In this way I will know that you have dealt graciously with my master."

When the servant arrives in Mesopotamia, he sets up a test for God. If the young woman is generous and strong, then she is the right one for Isaac. Thus this is to be a marriage made in heaven. God decides who the bride will be. God's choice of this woman is a sign of God's covenant love (in Hebrew, *hesed*) for Isaac (24:14). Marriage is one of the Bible's favorite images for the covenant between God and the people. Just as Isaac is a sign of God's covenant with Abraham, so his wife will be a sign of God's faithful covenant love.

Genesis 24:15-33

¹⁵He had scarcely finished speaking when Rebekah—who was born to Bethuel, son of Milcah, the wife of Abraham's brother Nahor—came out with a jug on her shoulder. ¹⁶The young woman was very beautiful, a virgin, untouched by man. She went down to the spring and filled her jug. As she came up, ¹⁷the servant ran toward her and said, "Please give me a sip of water from your jug." ¹⁸"Drink, sir," she replied, and quickly lowering the jug into her hand, she gave him a drink. ¹⁹When she had finished giving him a drink, she said, "I will draw water for your camels, too, until they have finished drinking." ²⁰With that, she quickly emptied her jug into the drinking trough and ran back to the well to draw more water, until she had drawn enough for all the camels. ²¹The man watched her the whole time, silently waiting to learn whether or not the LORD had made his journey successful. ²²When the camels had finished drinking, the man took out a gold nose-ring weighing half a shekel, and two gold bracelets weighing ten shekels for her wrists. ²³Then he asked her: "Whose daughter are you? Tell me, please. And is there a place in your father's house for us to spend the night?" ²⁴She answered: "I am the daughter of Bethuel the son of Milcah, whom she bore to Nahor. ²⁵We have plenty of straw and fodder," she added, "and also a place to spend the night." ²⁶The man then knelt and bowed down to the LORD, ²⁷saying: "Blessed be the LORD, the God of my master Abraham, who has not let his kindness and fidelity toward my master fail. As for me, the LORD has led me straight to the house of my master's brother."

²⁸Then the young woman ran off and told her mother's household what had happened. ²⁹Now Rebekah had a brother named Laban. Laban rushed outside to the man at the spring. ³⁰When he saw the nose-ring and the bracelets on his sister's arms and when he heard Rebekah repeating what the man had said to her, he went to him while he was standing by the camels at the spring. ³¹He said: "Come, blessed of the LORD! Why are you standing outside when I have made the house ready, as well as a place for the camels?" ³²The man then went inside; and while the camels were being unloaded and provided with straw and fodder, water was brought to bathe his feet and the feet of the men who were with him. ³³But when food was set before him, he said, "I will not eat until I have told my story." "Go ahead," they replied.

These verses are characterized by haste. The servant has scarcely finished speaking when Rebekah arrives. She offers the servant a drink and quickly lowers her jug to give him water. She offers to water the camels, quickly empties the jug, and runs back and forth to the well until the camels are satisfied. All this time the servant watches her work, waits to see if she passes the test.

After the camels are watered, the servant gives Rebekah gold jewelry and asks her name. He is amazed that God has not only provided this generous and energetic young woman, but that she is one of Abraham's relatives. In these early stories, belonging to the same family or clan as the groom is an asset for the bride.

Rebekah offers the servant hospitality: "We have plenty of straw and fodder . . . and also a place to spend the night." Then she runs to tell her family. Her brother Laban, after he has seen the gold, runs to meet the stranger. The servant is in a hurry, too. He will not eat until he has accomplished his errand.

The servant then tells his story (Gen 24:34-48), repeating most of the details (one reason this chapter is so long), and states: "Now, if you will act with kindness and fidelity toward my master, let me know; but if not, let me know that too. I can then proceed accordingly." Laban then replies: "This thing comes from the LORD; we can say nothing to you either for or against it. Here is Rebekah, right in front of you; take her and go, that she may become the wife of your master's son, as the LORD has said" (24:50-51). As the story continues, the servant is eager to be off, but the family urges the servant to stay and celebrate for ten days (24:52-54).

Who will decide what Rebekah will do? Apparently Rebekah's brother and mother know that Rebekah makes up her own mind:

Genesis 24:54-67

When they got up the next morning, [Abraham's servant] said, "Allow me to return to my master." [55][Rebekah's] brother and mother replied, "Let the young woman stay with us a short while, say ten days; after that she may go." [56]But he said to them, "Do not detain me, now that the LORD has made my journey successful; let me go back to my master." [57]They answered, "Let us call the young woman and see what she herself has to say about it." [58]So they called Rebekah and asked her, "Will you go with this man?" She answered, "I will."

[59]At this they sent off their sister Rebekah and her nurse with Abraham's servant and his men. [60]They blessed Rebekah and said:

"Sister, may you grow
    into thousands of myriads;
And may your descendants gain possession
    of the gates of their enemies!"

[61]Then Rebekah and her attendants started out; they mounted the camels and followed the man. So the servant took Rebekah and went on his way.

[62]Meanwhile Isaac had gone from Beer-lahai-roi and was living in the region of the Negeb. [63]One day toward evening he went out to walk in the field, and caught sight of camels approaching. [64]Rebekah, too, caught sight of Isaac, and got down from her camel. [65]She asked the servant, "Who is the man over there, walking through the fields toward us?" "That is my master," replied the servant. Then she took her veil and covered herself.

[66]The servant recounted to Isaac all the things he had done. [67]Then Isaac brought Rebekah into the tent of his mother Sarah. He took Rebekah as his wife. Isaac loved her and found solace after the death of his mother.

The family invokes a blessing on Rebekah. This is the first story in Genesis that tells of one human being blessing another. It is fitting that the one blessed should be Rebekah. She will be instrumental in the next blessing scene.

A touching story closes the chapter. As the travelers arrive at their destination, Rebekah spies Isaac walking toward them. She ascertains his identity and covers herself with her veil. Isaac takes her into his mother's tent, and in his love for her, Isaac finds solace after the death of his mother Sarah.

Rebekah is a worthy daughter-in-law of Sarah. She is beautiful, strong, generous, and willing to work. She is a woman of decision, capable of acting on the decision at the moment. She is willing, as Abraham and Sarah were, to leave homeland and family. She leaves not only for a land she has never seen, but for a husband she has never seen. She is brave. God has chosen a husband for her and she runs to accomplish her part. God has chosen a good wife for Isaac, child of promise.

Descendants

Genesis 25:19-26

[19] These are the descendants of Isaac, son of Abraham; Abraham begot Isaac. [20] Isaac was forty years old when he married Rebekah, the daughter of Bethuel the Aramean of Paddan-aram and the sister of Laban the Aramean. [21] Isaac entreated the LORD on behalf of his wife, since she was sterile. The LORD heard his entreaty, and his wife Rebekah became pregnant. [22] But the children jostled each other in the womb so much that she exclaimed, "If it is like this, why go on living!" She went to consult the LORD, [23] and the LORD answered her:

Two nations are in your womb,
    two peoples are separating while still
        within you;
But one will be stronger than the other,
    and the older will serve the younger.

[24] When the time of her delivery came, there were twins in her womb. [25] The first to emerge was reddish, and his whole body was like a hairy mantle; so they named him Esau. [26] Next his brother came out, gripping Esau's heel; so he was named Jacob. Isaac was sixty years old when they were born.

Again we have the story of a woman who is barren whose child is to be the child of promise. Rebekah, however, conceives twins: Esau, the hairy elder, and Jacob, the crafty younger. The struggle between the two begins in the womb. Rebekah is as decisive with God as she is in human encounters. She herself goes to seek God's word. She complains about her difficult pregnancy, saying, "If it is like this, why go

on living!" God hears her complaint and answers her. The response does not alleviate her physical distress but explains its reason. The two children will become the fathers of two nations, the people of Edom and the people of Israel (see Gen 25:30; 32:29). The twins' struggle in the womb represents the struggle of nations. A subsequent verse indicates that Isaac prefers Esau while Rebekah prefers Jacob (25:28). The parents' preferences seem insignificant, but the blessing scene to come will prove otherwise.

Wife-Sister Story

Genesis 26:6-11

[6] So Isaac settled in Gerar. [7] When the men of the place asked questions about his wife, he answered, "She is my sister." He was afraid that, if he called her his wife, the men of the place would kill him on account of Rebekah, since she was beautiful. [8] But when they had been there for a long time, Abimelech, king of the Philistines, looked out of a window and saw Isaac fondling his wife Rebekah. [9] He called for Isaac and said: "She must certainly be your wife! How could you have said, 'She is my sister'?" Isaac replied, "I thought I might lose my life on her account." [10] "How could you have done this to us!" exclaimed Abimelech. "It would have taken very little for one of the people to lie with your wife, and so you would have brought guilt upon us!" [11] Abimelech then commanded all the people: "Anyone who maltreats this man or his wife shall be put to death."

This is the third wife-sister story. The two preceding stories (Gen 12:10-20; 20:1-18) concern Sarah and Abraham. The plot is similar in all three stories. There are some significant variations, however, in this third story. First of all, Rebekah is younger in the story than Sarah, thus heightening the danger to her husband. Secondly, Abimelech (see Gen 20:1-18) discovers the deception in a much more natural fashion. He sees the husband caressing his wife. Thirdly, the Hebrew word translated here as "fondling" is *mesaheq*, from the same root as Isaac's name (*yishaq*), a root that means "laughter, play."[5] There is a pun in the story: Abimelech sees Isaac "Isaac-ing" his wife.

If we consider the three wife-sister stories in Genesis, we see Rebekah suffering the same humiliation as Sarah. Both women are denied by their husbands. Rebekah is described again as very beautiful (see Gen 24:16). She, like Sarah, holds life and death.

Blessing

Genesis 27:1-17

[1]When Isaac was so old that his eyesight had failed him, he called his older son Esau and said to him, "My son!" "Here I am!" he replied. [2]Isaac then said, "Now I have grown old. I do not know when I might die. [3]So now take your hunting gear—your quiver and bow—and go out into the open country to hunt some game for me. [4]Then prepare for me a dish in the way I like, and bring it to me to eat, so that I may bless you before I die."

[5]Rebekah had been listening while Isaac was speaking to his son Esau. So when Esau went out into the open country to hunt some game for his father, [6]Rebekah said to her son Jacob, "Listen! I heard your father tell your brother Esau, [7]'Bring me some game and prepare a dish for me to eat, that I may bless you with the LORD's approval before I die.' [8]Now, my son, obey me in what I am about to order you. [9]Go to the flock and get me two choice young goats so that with these I might prepare a dish for your father in the way he likes. [10]Then bring it to your father to eat, that he may bless you before he dies." [11]But Jacob said to his mother Rebekah, "But my brother Esau is a hairy man and I am smooth-skinned! [12]Suppose my father feels me? He will think I am making fun of him, and I will bring on myself a curse instead of a blessing." [13]His mother, however, replied: "Let any curse against you, my son, fall on me! Just obey me. Go and get me the young goats."

[14]So Jacob went and got them and brought them to his mother, and she prepared a dish in the way his father liked. [15]Rebekah then took the best clothes of her older son Esau that she had in the house, and gave them to her younger son Jacob to wear; [16]and with the goatskins she covered up his hands and the hairless part of his neck. [17]Then she gave her son Jacob the dish and the bread she had prepared.

As the story of the *birth* of Isaac is primary for Sarah, the story of the *blessing* of Jacob is the most significant concerning Rebekah. In this passage she, not Isaac, makes the decision concerning which son will continue as God's covenant partner. Rebekah herself was blessed by her mother and brother (see Gen 24:60). In her initial appearance in the biblical narrative, she shows herself to be quick and strong-minded (24:18-20, 58). Rebekah prefers Jacob to Esau (25:28). She has already heard God's word that the elder will serve the younger (25:23). Her action will confirm the choice.

In the ancient world every achievement and every failure was seen as a direct result of some form of divine intervention. In the Old Testament, **words of blessing** became a tool that called forth divine intervention in the life of an individual or in the world at large. The words themselves took on a life of their own; their power was not magic but was the result of God's life in them. Because of this divine power, a blessing could not be reversed or taken away. The same was true for words that cursed.

Rebekah, having overheard Isaac's plan to bless Esau, concocts a plan to substitute Jacob for the favored son. She will prepare a meal that Isaac likes. (The appetizing meal is mentioned three times: 27:9, 14, 17!) She will disguise Jacob as Esau. When Jacob is afraid that his father will discover him and give him a curse instead of a blessing, his mother Rebekah says, "Let any curse against you, my son, fall on me!" She will sacrifice anything for her beloved son.

Rebekah's plan succeeds. Isaac, initially suspicious, is reassured and blesses Jacob with a wonderful blessing (27:18-29). When Esau comes with his own appetizing dish, he is too late. All he can get is a half-hearted blessing which amounts to a curse (27:30-40).

Mother and Sons

Genesis 27:41-46

⁴¹Esau bore a grudge against Jacob because of the blessing his father had given him. Esau said to himself, "Let the time of mourning for my father come, so that I may kill my brother Jacob." ⁴²When Rebekah got news of what her older son Esau had in mind, she summoned her younger son Jacob and said to him: "Listen! Your brother Esau intends to get his revenge by killing you. ⁴³So now, my son, obey me: flee at once to my brother Laban in Haran, ⁴⁴and stay with him a while until your brother's fury subsides— ⁴⁵until your brother's anger against you subsides and he forgets what you did to him. Then

I will send for you and bring you back. Why should I lose both of you in a single day?"

⁴⁶Rebekah said to Isaac: "I am disgusted with life because of the Hittite women. If Jacob also should marry a Hittite woman, a native of the land, like these women, why should I live?"

In Rebekah's final scene she protects her younger son from her elder son, as Esau is ready to kill Jacob because of the blessing. Rebekah solves the problem indirectly. She proposes to Isaac that Jacob go back to Haran to find a wife. To Jacob, however, she clearly explains the planned journey as flight from the murderous Esau. Isaac follows Rebekah's suggestion and sends Jacob back to the house of Bethuel. As Jacob departs, Isaac blesses him again, this time with full recognition (Gen 28:1-5).

According to the traditions recorded in Genesis, Rebekah does not see her favored son again. Her death is not reported, but she is not mentioned when Jacob finally returns to the house of Isaac (Gen 35:27). She and Isaac are buried in Hebron (the cave in Machpelah) with Abraham and Sarah (Gen 49:31). As a matriarch, Rebekah was instrumental in mothering, choosing, and orchestrating Jacob as a child of blessing.

More Women of the Old Testament

Potiphar's Wife

The women in this lesson all have a close connection to Jacob, but there are a few other women in the surrounding narratives. One of them is Potiphar's wife (Gen 39), who is found in the narratives about Joseph, one of Jacob's sons. While Joseph is in Egypt, having been sold by his brothers, an Egyptian official named Potiphar purchases Joseph and has him work in his home. The official's wife tries to engage in sexual activity with Joseph on multiple occasions, commanding him to lie with her, but he refuses. Ultimately, Potiphar's wife falsely states that Joseph propositioned her, and she uses his cloak to support her false claim. Her actions land Joseph in prison, where God remains with him and helps him to survive and thrive in Egypt.

—*Jaime L. Waters*

LEAH AND RACHEL

Betrothal

Genesis 29:9-14

[9]While [Jacob] was still talking with [the shepherds], Rachel arrived with her father's sheep, for she was the one who tended them. [10]As soon as Jacob saw Rachel, the daughter of his mother's brother Laban, and the sheep of Laban, he went up, rolled the stone away from the mouth of the well, and watered Laban's sheep. [11]Then Jacob kissed Rachel and wept aloud. [12]Jacob told Rachel that he was her father's relative, Rebekah's son. So she ran to tell her father. [13]When Laban heard the news about Jacob, his sister's son, he ran to meet him. After embracing and kissing him, he brought him to his house. Jacob then repeated to Laban all these things, [14]and Laban said to him, "You are indeed my bone and my flesh."

The story of Jacob's meeting with Rachel is another betrothal type scene, sharing similarities with the events described in Genesis 24 (Isaac and Rebekah). Most of the elements are present: a stranger, a young woman, a well, drawing water, and a sense of haste. The variations in the story reveal Jacob's passionate nature. At the sight of Rachel, he alone rolls the massive stone from the mouth of the well. Then he kisses his cousin and bursts into tears. It is indeed a story of love at first sight!

Two Sisters

Genesis 29:14-20

After Jacob had stayed with him a full month, [15]Laban said to him: "Should you serve me for nothing just because you are a relative of mine? Tell me what your wages should be." [16]Now Laban had two daughters; the older was called Leah, the younger Rachel. [17]Leah had dull eyes, but Rachel was shapely and beautiful. [18]Because Jacob loved Rachel, he answered, "I will serve you seven years for your younger daughter Rachel." [19]Laban replied, "It is better to give her to you than to another man. Stay with me." [20]So Jacob served seven years for Rachel, yet they seemed to him like a few days because of his love for her.

Laban's two daughters are named Leah, meaning "wearied," and Rachel, meaning "ewe." They are identified as elder and younger sisters. Again we are given more information than seems necessary. The added information, however, is crucial for the plot of the story. We are told that Rachel is "shapely and beautiful," confirming the reasons for Jacob's love. There is something noteworthy, however, about Leah's eyes. The word describing them, *rakkoth*, means "tender," "gentle," "frail," "delicate," "weak." It has sometimes been interpreted as indicating weak or watery eyes; it is sometimes translated as "lovely."[6] It has been suggested that perhaps Leah had blue eyes (a strange occurrence in the Middle East). Blue eyes can be more sensitive to light (thus watery), and are more likely to be nearsighted (thus "weak"). They can certainly also be lovely! Jacob's love for Rachel makes him willing to serve Laban seven years for her, a generous bride-price. But the years seem as nothing because of the strength of his passion.

Marriage

Genesis 29:21-30

[21]Then Jacob said to Laban, "Give me my wife, that I may consummate my marriage with her, for my term is now completed." [22]So Laban invited all the local inhabitants and gave a banquet. [23]At nightfall he took his daughter Leah and brought her to Jacob, and he consummated the marriage with her. [24]Laban assigned his maidservant Zilpah

to his daughter Leah as her maidservant. [25]In the morning, there was Leah! So Jacob said to Laban: "How could you do this to me! Was it not for Rachel that I served you? Why did you deceive me?" [26]Laban replied, "It is not the custom in our country to give the younger daughter before the firstborn. [27]Finish the bridal week for this one, and then the other will also be given to you in return for another seven years of service with me."

[28]Jacob did so. He finished the bridal week for the one, and then Laban gave him his daughter Rachel as a wife. [29]Laban assigned his maidservant Bilhah to his daughter Rachel as her maidservant. [30]Jacob then consummated his marriage with Rachel also, and he loved her more than Leah. Thus he served Laban another seven years.

The story of Jacob's marriage to Rachel and Leah is a story of the deceiver deceived. Jacob, the younger brother, schemed to steal the blessing from Esau, the elder. Jacob serves Laban seven years to marry Rachel, the younger sister, and instead is given Leah, the elder. Rachel costs him another seven years.

The story may be poetic justice for Jacob. One can only imagine the sorrow and pain it presents to the two sisters. Leah can have no doubt that her husband loves her sister more. Rachel suffers the indignity of seeing her sister celebrate and consummate what was, to be her own marriage with a man who loves her passionately. The seeds of strife are planted between the two sisters, and they seem powerless to change the course of events.

Descendants

Genesis 29:31–30:13

[31]When the LORD saw that Leah was unloved, he made her fruitful, while Rachel was barren. [32]Leah conceived and bore a son, and she named him Reuben; for she said, "It means, 'The LORD saw my misery; surely now my husband will love me.'" [33]She conceived again and bore a son, and said, "It means, 'The LORD heard that I was unloved,' and therefore he has given me this one

continue

Jacob and Rachel meet at the well. Julius Schnorr von Carolsfeld (1860).

also"; so she named him Simeon. [34]Again she conceived and bore a son, and she said, "Now at last my husband will become attached to me, since I have now borne him three sons"; that is why she named him Levi. [35]Once more she conceived and bore a son, and she said, "This time I will give thanks to the LORD"; therefore she named him Judah. Then she stopped bearing children.

[30:1]When Rachel saw that she had not borne children to Jacob, she became envious of her sister. She said to Jacob, "Give me children or I shall die!" [2]Jacob became angry with Rachel and said, "Can I take the place of God, who has denied you the fruit of the womb?" [3]She replied, "Here is my maidservant Bilhah. Have intercourse with her, and let her give birth on my knees, so that I too may have children through her." [4]So she gave him her maidservant Bilhah as wife, and Jacob had intercourse with her. [5]When Bilhah conceived and bore a son for Jacob, [6]Rachel said, "God has vindicated me; indeed he has heeded my plea and given me a son." Therefore she named him Dan. [7]Rachel's maidservant Bilhah conceived again and bore a second son for Jacob, [8]and Rachel said, "I have wrestled strenuously with my sister, and I have prevailed." So she named him Naphtali.

[9]When Leah saw that she had ceased to bear children, she took her maidservant Zilpah and gave her to Jacob as wife. [10]So Leah's maidservant Zilpah bore a son for Jacob. [11]Leah then said, "What good luck!" So she named him Gad. [12]Then Leah's maidservant Zilpah bore a second son to Jacob; [13]and Leah said, "What good fortune, because women will call me fortunate!" So she named him Asher.

Genesis 29:31–30:24 chronicles the struggle between the two sisters, Leah and Rachel, over who can give birth to Jacob's children. Leah is fruitful but unloved; Rachel is loved but barren. Leah gives birth to four sons: Reuben, Simeon, Levi, and Judah. In despair Rachel demands of Jacob: "Give me children or I shall die!" Jacob, in hot anger, retorts: "Can I take the

place of God?" So Rachel turns to the same solution that Sarah tried, surrogate motherhood through her maidservant. After Bilhah bears two sons for Rachel, Dan and Naphtali, Leah also gives her maidservant to Jacob. Zilpah also bears two sons for Leah: Gad and Asher.

The mothers' interpretations of their sons' names indicate the progress of the struggle between the two sisters. Leah's first four sons are named Reuben (the Lord saw my misery), Simeon (the Lord heard that I was unloved), Levi (now my husband will become attached to me), and Judah (I will give grateful praise). Rachel's sons through Bilhah are Dan (God has vindicated me) and Naphtali (I have wrestled with my sister and prevailed). Leah responds with the names of her sons through Zilpah: Gad (what good luck!) and Asher (women call me fortunate).

Genesis 30:14-24

[14]One day, during the wheat harvest, Reuben went out and came upon some mandrakes in the field which he brought home to his mother Leah. Rachel said to Leah, "Please give me some of your son's mandrakes." [15]Leah replied, "Was it not enough for you to take away my husband, that you must now take my son's mandrakes too?" Rachel answered, "In that case Jacob may lie with you tonight in exchange for your son's mandrakes." [16]That evening, when Jacob came in from the field, Leah went out to meet him. She said, "You must have intercourse with me, because I have hired you with my son's mandrakes." So that night he lay with her, [17]and God listened to Leah; she conceived and bore a fifth son to Jacob. [18]Leah then said, "God has given me my wages for giving my maidservant to my husband"; so she named him Issachar. [19]Leah conceived again and bore a sixth son to Jacob; [20]and Leah said, "God has brought me a precious gift. This time my husband will honor me, because I have borne him six sons";

so she named him Zebulun. ²¹Afterwards she gave birth to a daughter, and she named her Dinah.

²²Then God remembered Rachel. God listened to her and made her fruitful. ²³She conceived and bore a son, and she said, "God has removed my disgrace." ²⁴She named him Joseph, saying, "May the LORD add another son for me!"

Still the contest continues. Rachel has access to Jacob because he loves her; Leah is still ahead in the number of sons. So the sisters make a bargain. Rachel trades a night with Jacob for mandrakes that Leah's son has gathered. Mandrakes were considered a fertility drug in the ancient world. The bargain suggests cooperation between the two sisters, although the sharp language reveals the tension between them.

The trade seems to work for both sisters. Leah gives birth to Issachar (God has given me my reward) and subsequently to Zebulun (my husband will offer me presents). Leah now has six sons of her own and two through Zilpah. Finally God remembers Rachel. She, too, gives birth to a son, her firstborn, whom she names Joseph (may the Lord add another). Rachel now has one son of her own and two through Bilhah. Her sister has prevailed in the struggle. Eight of Jacob's eleven sons are Leah's; only three are Rachel's. Leah has more than her share of the twelve future tribes.

 The **stigma of barrenness** in the Old Testament stems from a variety of social and religious roots, including childbearing as an expected role for women in the ancient world, and God's command to both men and women at creation: "Be fertile and multiply" (Gen 1:28). Barrenness was therefore seen as a burden, an embarrassment, or even a curse. Of course, in a modern context, we view the physiological situation of infertility and the larger context of women's roles in society much differently.

Departure from Haran

Meanwhile, as the sisters struggle with each other, Jacob struggles with Laban for wealth. No matter what terms Laban sets, Jacob wins. "So the man grew exceedingly prosperous, and he owned large flocks, male and female servants, camels, and donkeys" (Gen 30:43). Laban's sons are not happy with Jacob's increasing prosperity. The fourteen years of service are long over. So Jacob sends for Rachel and Leah and reports to them the tension between himself and Laban and his sons. He also tells them of a dream in which God commands him to return to the land of his birth.

Genesis 31:14-35

¹⁴Rachel and Leah answered him: "Do we still have an heir's portion in our father's house? ¹⁵Are we not regarded by him as outsiders? He not only sold us; he has even used up the money that he got for us! ¹⁶All the wealth that God took away from our father really belongs to us and our children. So do whatever God has told you." ¹⁷Jacob proceeded to put his children and wives on camels, ¹⁸and he drove off all his livestock and all the property he had acquired in Paddan-aram, to go to his father Isaac in the land of Canaan.

¹⁹Now Laban was away shearing his sheep, and Rachel had stolen her father's household images. ²⁰Jacob had hoodwinked Laban the Aramean by not telling him that he was going to flee. ²¹Thus he fled with all that he had. Once he was across the Euphrates, he headed for the hill country of Gilead.

²²On the third day, word came to Laban that Jacob had fled. ²³Taking his kinsmen with him, he pursued him for seven days until he caught up with him in the hill country of Gilead. ²⁴But that night God appeared to Laban the Aramean in a dream and said to him: Take care not to say anything to Jacob.

²⁵When Laban overtook Jacob, Jacob's tents were pitched in the hill country; Laban also

continue

pitched his tents in the hill country of Gilead. [26]Laban said to Jacob, "How could you hoodwink me and carry off my daughters like prisoners of war? [27]Why did you dupe me by stealing away secretly? You did not tell me! I would have sent you off with joyful singing to the sound of tambourines and harps. [28]You did not even allow me a parting kiss to my daughters and grandchildren! Now what you have done makes no sense. [29]I have it in my power to harm all of you; but last night the God of your father said to me, 'Take care not to say anything to Jacob!' [30]Granted that you had to leave because you were longing for your father's house, why did you steal my gods?" [31]Jacob replied to Laban, "I was frightened at the thought that you might take your daughters away from me by force. [32]As for your gods, the one you find them with shall not remain alive! If, with our kinsmen looking on, you identify anything here as belonging to you, take it." Jacob had no idea that Rachel had stolen the household images.

[33]Laban then went in and searched Jacob's tent and Leah's tent, as well as the tents of the two maidservants; but he did not find them. Leaving Leah's tent, he went into Rachel's. [34]Meanwhile Rachel had taken the household images, put them inside the camel's saddlebag, and seated herself upon them. When Laban had rummaged through her whole tent without finding them, [35]she said to her father, "Do not let my lord be angry that I cannot rise in your presence; I am having my period." So, despite his search, he did not find the household images.

Rachel and Leah are as willing to leave family and homeland as were Sarah and Rebekah. So they and their children and maidservants depart with Jacob to return to Canaan. Rachel, however, took her father's household idols, thus removing the symbols of Laban's authority. Laban's pursuit of Jacob seems to be motivated primarily by the loss of the household gods. Jacob, innocent of the theft, pledges that the culprit will die, and Laban searches the tents of all the women. Rachel, however, has hidden the idols in a camel cushion and is sitting on them. She apologizes for not standing when her father enters; her excuse is her menstrual period. So Laban does not find the gods and makes peace with the departing Jacob.

Rachel's reasons for stealing the household idols are never stated. Is it her way of getting even with the father who so long ago denied her the wedding night? Is it her claim to Laban's property? In any case, Rachel proves herself adept at deception, similar to her aunt/mother-in-law Rebekah, her father Laban, and her husband Jacob. Rachel's claim of menstrual discomfort, whether true or not, subtly declares the uncleanness of the idols. Anything on which a menstruating woman sits is made unclean and anyone who touches anything on which she sits is also made unclean (Lev 15:19-24). Idols are unclean by definition. Rachel's action underlines that fact.

Birth and Death

Genesis 35:16-20

[16]Then they departed from Bethel; but while they still had some distance to go to Ephrath, Rachel went into labor and suffered great distress. [17]When her labor was most intense, the midwife said to her, "Do not fear, for now you have another son." [18]With her last breath—for she was at the point of death—she named him Ben-oni; but his father named him Benjamin. [19]Thus Rachel died; and she was buried on the road to Ephrath (now Bethlehem). [20]Jacob set up a sacred pillar on her grave, and the same pillar marks Rachel's grave to this day.

Jacob continues his journey home (Gen 32). When he meets Esau, he is afraid of his anger. But Esau is peaceful; the whole family survives (Gen 33).

While they are still on the journey Rachel goes into labor. She gives birth to a second son, but the childbirth has been too much for her. She dies and is buried on the road to Ephrath, which is interpreted as Bethlehem (see also Gen 48:7). There are two traditional sites for the tomb of Rachel, one just outside Bethlehem as this text indicates, and the other at Ramah, five or six miles north of Jerusalem (1 Sam 10:2; Jer 31:15). There is still a tomb of Rachel near Bethlehem.

Rachel names her son Ben-oni. Jacob names him Benjamin. What do these two names mean? The Hebrew word ôn means "strength," frequently referring to the power of fertility (Gen 49:3; Deut 21:17; Job 40:16; Pss 78:51; 105:36).[7] Rachel had earlier asked for another son (Gen 30:24). She names this second son "the son of my strength." Jacob confirms the name by calling the child *ben-yamin*, "son of my right hand." Or should we interpret Jacob's naming to mean that Rachel is his right hand?

The Memory of Leah and Rachel

There are a few other significant texts in which Rachel and/or Leah are mentioned. In his farewell discourse Jacob says that he buried Leah in Hebron, in the cave where Abraham and Sarah, Isaac and Rebekah are buried. Jacob wishes to be buried there with her (Gen 49:28-32). The unloved wife lies with the husband in death. The descendants of the unloved wife also become more powerful than those of the beloved wife. Leah's son Judah is the ancestor of David (1 Sam 17:12; Sir 45:25) and thus of Jesus (Matt 1:3-6; Luke 3:30-32).

Rachel's descendants, the Rachel tribes of Benjamin and of Joseph's sons Ephraim and Manasseh, do not survive through the centuries of Israel's history. The tribe of Benjamin is absorbed into Judah. Ephraim and Manasseh (along with Dan and Naphtali, Rachel's tribes through Bilhah) are taken captive by the Assyrians in the eighth century and do not return. Jeremiah, reporting the Assyrian captivity, describes the sorrow of Rachel: "Thus says the LORD: / In Ramah is heard the sound of sobbing, bitter weeping! / Rachel mourns for her children, she refuses to be consoled / For her children—they are no more" (Jer 31:15).

Matthew borrows this text to tell the story of Herod's attempt to kill the infant Jesus by slaughtering the baby boys of Bethlehem (Matt 2:18). Note that the Jeremiah text is based on the tradition that Rachel was buried in Ramah, and the Matthew text on the tradition that she was buried near Bethlehem.

The sisters together become a blessing for future mothers in Israel. When Ruth marries Boaz, the people say, "May the LORD make this woman come into your house like Rachel and Leah, who between them built up the house of Israel. Prosper in Ephrathah! Bestow a name in Bethlehem!" (Ruth 4:11). Ruth becomes the mother of Obed, the grandfather of David.

Who are Leah and Rachel?

The two sisters, Rachel and Leah, wives of Jacob, have a complicated story. Their lives are marked by tragedy: Leah is unloved, Rachel is barren and then dies in childbirth. They are set in opposition to one another, and yet there are evidences of cooperation between them. They are the mothers of Israel, the biological mothers of eight of the tribal ancestors and the adoptive mothers of the other four. Jacob favors Rachel's children, Joseph and Benjamin, but in the long view of history it is Leah's son, Judah, who will prevail. Two sisters—both necessary for the story, both major influences on the history of Israel.

DEBORAH

Rebekah's Nurse

Genesis 24:59; 35:8

[59]At this they sent off their sister Rebekah and her nurse with Abraham's servant and his men. . . .

[8]Deborah, Rebekah's nurse, died. She was buried under the oak below Bethel, and so it was named Allon-bacuth.

Rebekah's nurse is mentioned only twice. When Rebekah leaves her family house, her nurse goes with her. Deborah must have been a young woman when they left Haran.[8] She, too, is uprooted from her native place, her only security being her relationship with her mistress Rebekah.

The notice of her death raises several questions. Why does it seem that she is returning from Haran with Jacob at the time of her death? Did Rebekah send Deborah to Jacob? Was she sent to help his wives with their children? Did Isaac send her home when Rebekah died? Is this a different woman? Is the verse misplaced?

It is also noteworthy that the tree beneath which she is buried is named Allon-bacuth, "the oak of weeping." Does the name of the tree recall the grief at the death of this faithful old woman? Does the weeping indicate how much she was loved by the children and grandchildren of her mistress? Does she give both her name and her tree to another Deborah, judge of Israel (Judg 4:4-5)?

BILHAH AND ZILPAH
Servants of Rachel and Leah

Genesis 29:24, 29

[24]Laban assigned his maidservant Zilpah to his daughter Leah as her maidservant. . . . [29]Laban assigned his maidservant Bilhah to his daughter Rachel as her maidservant.

The two maidservants of Rachel and Leah, Zilpah and Bilhah, are assigned to their mistresses at the time of their marriage. The announcement is made in identical language. The two women are barely distinguished; they are given no personality. Bilhah and Zilpah are given to Jacob as surrogate mothers by Rachel and Leah (Gen 30:3-12), just as Hagar was given to Abraham by Sarah. The transaction here, however, seems more successful. The sons of Bilhah and Zilpah are adopted by Rachel and Leah and are regarded as members of the family, in contrast to the treatment of Ishmael by Sarah. The two maidservants

are regularly listed in the genealogies along with their sons (Gen 35:25-26; 46:18, 25). They are the biological mothers of four of the tribes of Israel: Dan and Naphtali, Gad and Asher.

The status of Bilhah and Zilpah, however, is never forgotten. When Jacob meets Esau, he puts the two maidservants and their children in front (Gen 33:1-2). If Esau should attack, these women and their children who are least valued by Jacob will absorb the blow and perhaps protect Leah and Rachel. Bilhah suffers one further tragedy. When Jacob was returning to Canaan, "Reuben went and lay with Bilhah, his father's concubine" (Gen 35:22). Jacob is offended and diminishes Reuben's blessing (Gen 49:3-4), but there is no word of concern for Bilhah, the powerless maidservant.

These two women, Zilpah and Bilhah, were servants and pawns in the struggle for sons, yet they gave birth to one-third of the tribes of Israel.

DINAH
Rape and Massacre

Genesis 34:1-7, 24-31

[1]Dinah, the daughter whom Leah had borne to Jacob, went out to visit some of the women of the land. [2]When Shechem, son of Hamor the Hivite, the leader of the region, saw her, he seized her and lay with her by force. [3]He was strongly attracted to Dinah, daughter of Jacob, and was in love with the young woman. So he spoke affectionately to her. [4]Shechem said to his father Hamor, "Get me this young woman for a wife."

[5]Meanwhile, Jacob heard that Shechem had defiled his daughter Dinah; but since his sons were out in the field with his livestock, Jacob kept quiet until they came home. [6]Now Hamor, the father of Shechem, went out to discuss the matter with Jacob, [7]just as Jacob's sons were coming in from the field. When they heard the news, the men were indignant and extremely angry. Shechem had committed an outrage in Israel by lying with Jacob's daughter; such a thing is not done. . . .

²⁴All who went out of the gate of the city listened to Hamor and his son Shechem, and all the males, all those who went out of the gate of the city, were circumcised. ²⁵On the third day, while they were still in pain, two of Jacob's sons, Simeon and Levi, brothers of Dinah, each took his sword, advanced against the unsuspecting city and massacred all the males. ²⁶After they had killed Hamor and his son Shechem with the sword, they took Dinah from Shechem's house and left. ²⁷Then the other sons of Jacob followed up the slaughter and sacked the city because their sister had been defiled. ²⁸They took their sheep, cattle and donkeys, whatever was in the city and in the surrounding country. ²⁹They carried off all their wealth, their children, and their women, and looted whatever was in the houses.

³⁰Jacob said to Simeon and Levi: "You have brought trouble upon me by making me repugnant to the inhabitants of the land, the Canaanites and the Perizzites. I have so few men that, if these people unite against me and attack me, I and my household will be wiped out." ³¹But they retorted, "Should our sister be treated like a prostitute?"

Dinah is the daughter of Leah and Jacob (Gen 30:21; cf. 46:15). She is the only daughter of Jacob named. She is mentioned no doubt because of this story in Genesis 34.

Dinah's story is a story of rape and vengeance. It is a story of men's power and passion. The feelings of Dinah are never described. She suffers the violence of rape. Shechem, whose name is also the name of a place, is reported to be "in love" with her, then wants to marry her (34:3-4, 8, 11-12, 19). Is she revolted by the thought of marriage to this violent man? Was she in love with him before the rape? Does she feel betrayed? Why is she staying in Shechem's house (34:26)? Is she imprisoned or is it her choice? We are told nothing.

Dinah's full brothers, Simeon and Levi, are outraged. First they deceive the men of Shechem; then they slaughter them. They do all this because their sister Dinah has been "defiled" (34:5, 13). After the massacre, they take Dinah from Shechem's house and leave. Then the rest of Jacob's sons pillage the city "because their sister had been defiled" (34:27). Jacob is not happy about their actions, but they reply, "Should our sister be treated like a prostitute?" (34:31).

Dinah has been friendly with the women of the land (34:1). Does the slaughter of the city and the capture of the women and children grieve her? Her brothers now regard her as "defiled," and the incident has marked her with the word "prostitute." Will she ever have honor in the family again? Will she ever be allowed to marry? Dinah's fate is not the concern of the story. The narrator, unfortunately, is more interested in the defeat of Shechem by Simeon and Levi.

In these early stories of Israel's leaders, women often appear only to further the story, leaving their **character development or fate** to the listener's or reader's imagination. This is especially true of female servants like Deborah who must stay in her mistress' good favor to survive; Bilhah and Zilpah who had little choice but to bear children for a clan's leader; and women like Dinah who are "defiled" and, through no fault of their own, bring shame to their families.

TAMAR

A Righteous Woman

Genesis 38:6-30

⁶Judah got a wife named Tamar for his firstborn, Er. ⁷But Er, Judah's firstborn, greatly offended the LORD; so the LORD took his life. ⁸Then Judah said to Onan, "Have intercourse with your brother's wife, in fulfillment of your duty as brother-in-law, and thus preserve your brother's line." ⁹Onan, however, knew that the offspring would not be his; so whenever he had intercourse

continue

with his brother's wife, he wasted his seed on the ground, to avoid giving offspring to his brother. [10]What he did greatly offended the LORD, and the LORD took his life too. [11]Then Judah said to his daughter-in-law Tamar, "Remain a widow in your father's house until my son Shelah grows up"—for he feared that Shelah also might die like his brothers. So Tamar went to live in her father's house.

[12]Time passed, and the daughter of Shua, Judah's wife, died. After Judah completed the period of mourning, he went up to Timnah, to those who were shearing his sheep, in company with his friend Hirah the Adullamite. [13]Then Tamar was told, "Your father-in-law is on his way up to Timnah to shear his sheep." [14]So she took off her widow's garments, covered herself with a shawl, and having wrapped herself sat down at the entrance to Enaim, which is on the way to Timnah; for she was aware that, although Shelah was now grown up, she had not been given to him in marriage. [15]When Judah saw her, he thought she was a harlot, since she had covered her face. [16]So he went over to her at the roadside and said, "Come, let me have intercourse with you," for he did not realize that she was his daughter-in-law. She replied, "What will you pay me for letting you have intercourse with me?" [17]He answered, "I will send you a young goat from the flock." "Very well," she said, "provided you leave me a pledge until you send it." [18]Judah asked, "What pledge should I leave you?" She answered, "Your seal and cord, and the staff in your hand." So he gave them to her and had intercourse with her, and she conceived by him. [19]After she got up and went away,

she took off her shawl and put on her widow's garments again.

[20]Judah sent the young goat by his friend the Adullamite to recover the pledge from the woman; but he did not find her. [21]So he asked the men of that place, "Where is the prostitute, the one by the roadside in Enaim?" But they answered, "No prostitute has been here." [22]He went back to Judah and told him, "I did not find her; and besides, the men of the place said, 'No prostitute has been here.'" [23]"Let her keep the things," Judah replied; "otherwise we will become a laughingstock. After all, I did send her this young goat, but you did not find her."

[24]About three months later, Judah was told, "Your daughter-in-law Tamar has acted like a harlot and now she is pregnant from her harlotry." Judah said, "Bring her out; let her be burned." [25]But as she was being brought out, she sent word to her father-in-law, "It is by the man to whom these things belong that I am pregnant." Then she said, "See whose seal and cord and staff these are." [26]Judah recognized them and said, "She is in the right rather than I, since I did not give her to my son Shelah." He had no further sexual relations with her.

[27]When the time of her delivery came, there were twins in her womb. [28]While she was giving birth, one put out his hand; and the midwife took and tied a crimson thread on his hand, noting, "This one came out first." [29]But as he withdrew his hand, his brother came out; and she said, "What a breach you have made for yourself!" So he was called Perez. [30]Afterward his brother, who had the crimson thread on his hand, came out; he was called Zerah.

The story of Tamar is the story of another woman who uses deceptive means in order to ensure the succession of descendants. Tamar is given in marriage to Judah's son Er. When Er dies because of his sinfulness, she is given to his brother Onan. Onan does not want to honor the obligation to his dead brother, so God takes his life also.

Tamar is now doubly widowed. Judah has a third son but is afraid that marriage with

Tamar will be deadly for this son also. So Tamar is instructed to return to her father's house and wait. Tamar, however, is not free. She is promised to the third son, Shelah, and must marry him or no one.

Tamar waits for years. Judah apparently has no intention of honoring the obligation to his dead son Er. So Tamar takes matters into her own hands. She disguises herself and waits for Judah on the way to Timnah. Judah mistakes her for a prostitute, contracts with her, and has intercourse with her. Each of these statements is significant.

Judah mistakes Tamar for a "harlot" or temple prostitute. He sends the fee the next day, but the people of the place say, "No prostitute has been here." Later Tamar is accused of "playing the harlot." Nowhere does the text claim that she *is* a prostitute. The people in the story, however, mistake her for one.

Tamar contracts with Judah: intercourse for a fee. She is not interested in payment, however; she is interested in identification. Tamar asks for Judah's seal, cord, and staff. She is not available for the payment of the fee, so she keeps the pledge. These items will save her life when she is about to be executed for adultery.

Judah has intercourse with Tamar, and she conceives. In the midst of the stories of barren women, Tamar conceives immediately. She gives birth to twins, Perez and Zerah. She herself has provided descendants for her dead husband and continued the line of Judah.

Judah's response to the discovery that he is the man responsible for Tamar's pregnancy, a situation for which he is about to execute her, is the key to the story. Judah exclaims, "She is in the right rather than I" (38:26). Righteousness in the Bible is always based on relationship. Tamar has honored the demands of the relationship with her dead husband whereas Judah has not. Thus Tamar is more righteous than Judah. She has taken on the responsibility of another and been judged guilty because of it. She has taken unconventional risks, broken the accepted pattern, and been judged guilty because of it. Yet in the end she is judged to be more righteous than the other main character in the story because she has honored the demands of the relationship.

Tamar's son Perez is an ancestor of David. Tamar is thus an ancestor of Jesus, son of David of the tribe of Judah. She herself is mentioned in the genealogy of Jesus in Matthew (Matt 1:3).

Generations later, Boaz, husband of Ruth, will be blessed in Tamar's name: "With the offspring the LORD will give you from this young woman, may your house become like the house of Perez, whom Tamar bore to Judah" (Ruth 4:12). The stories of Tamar and Judah and Ruth and Boaz (see Lesson Five) have in common the practice of levirate marriage. This practice, which comes from the Latin word *levir* (brother-in-law), holds that if a woman becomes a widow, the surviving brother-in law or next closest kinsman is to marry her. The practice of levirate marriage served as a way to provide descendants for the dead man, protect property and ensure it remained within a particular tribe or family, and provide financial and social stability for the widow, who was often vulnerable and disenfranchised in Israelite society. The extent to which levirate marriage was practiced is unknown, but biblical tradition attests to resistance to the practice, likely based on economic and social reasons. Such resistance is evident in Judah not giving his third son to Tamar for fear that he might suffer a similar outcome as his first two sons. The book of Ruth also attests resistance when the nearest kinsman to Ruth declines to care for her and the land associated with her deceased husband due to concerns about finances and inheritance (see Ruth 4:3-6).

CONTINUING THE CONVERSATION

By Jaime L. Waters

Rebekah: Authority in Family

Ancient Israel has been described as a patriarchal society in which men were afforded power over women, but this assessment has been challenged as limited, overly simplistic, and one-dimensional by several contemporary scholars. Carol Meyers and Elisabeth Schüssler-Fiorenza, for example, have made compelling arguments for more nuanced and accurate ways of speaking about the past. In *Rediscovering Eve: Ancient Israelite Women in Context*, Meyers uses biblical and archaeological evidence to argue that ancient Israel was a *heterarchy*, a system in which no particular group dominated another group. Meyers recognizes the diverse ways that women exerted power and influence, especially in household management. In *But She Said: Feminist Practices of Biblical Interpretation*, Schüssler-Fiorenza describes ancient Israel as a *kyriarchy*, a system built on multiple types of domination and oppression. Kyriarchy recognizes intersecting power dynamics, such as gender, race, class, religion, and age.

Influence of Rebekah's Mother

The traditions about Rebekah in the book of Genesis are helpful for expanding how we think about the power and influence of women, especially in families. Both Rebekah and her mother exhibit power and control within their family units. Likewise, the narratives about Rebekah include other power dynamics, such as manipulation of Isaac as he ages.

In Genesis 24, Abraham sends a servant to search for a woman to marry his son, Isaac. The servant encounters Rebekah at a well, and she shows him hospitality, giving water to him and his camels. The servant determines that she is right for Isaac and presents Rebekah with

jewelry, which she understands as a marriage proposal. While Rebekah introduces herself as the daughter of Bethuel, her father, the text then describes her running to her mother's house (Hebrew *bet immah*; Gen 24:28). Rebekah's father Bethuel is in the narrative and talks with the servant and with Rebekah's brother, Laban. However, the home is referred to as her mother's home, showing her mother's status and authority in that space. Likewise, before Rebekah leaves, her mother and brother speak on her behalf, advocating for her to stay with them for a longer period of time. The role that Rebekah's mother plays clearly depicts her as having authority over her family and home.

Rebekah's Authority

As the narrative continues, Isaac and Rebekah marry and have children, Jacob and Esau. Rebekah prefers Jacob while Isaac prefers Esau, the firstborn son who is associated with hunting. Rebekah decides that she wants Jacob to receive a blessing over Esau, so she crafts a plan to deceive her husband. Multiple times Rebekah tells Jacob to listen to her and follow her orders. She instructs him to bring her game meat so that she can prepare a meal for Isaac. She gives Jacob some of Esau's clothing to wear and puts animal skins on Jacob so he feels hairy like Esau. When Jacob worries that he might be cursed because of his deception, Rebekah takes any curse onto herself. Their deception works. Isaac in his old age believes Jacob is Esau, although he is suspicious of the interaction. Rebekah also intercedes to protect Jacob from Esau's wrath.

While Rebekah's orchestrating deception could be worthy of critique, her actions show her exercising authority within the family and household. She exercises power as mother of the household; her control also intersects with power dynamics related to aging, as she and Jacob fool Isaac in his old age. Rebekah sets into motion the privileging of Jacob, whose name is eventually changed to Israel. The descendants of Jacob/Israel, the Israelites, enter into a covenantal relationship with God. Rebekah's authoritative actions to secure the blessing of Jacob have positive effects on the people of Israel.

EXPLORING LESSON TWO

1. The arrival and testimony of a stranger seem to convince Rebekah and her family that God is at work (Gen 24:28-58). When has another person's faith and testimony been helpful for you or convinced you that God is present in your life?

_____

_____

_____

_____

_____

2. What are some of the ways Rebekah manipulates her family to assure that God's word to her would come to pass (Gen 25:23; 27:1-45)?

_____

_____

_____

_____

_____

3. How do you feel about Jacob being deceived, especially given his own past deception of Isaac (Gen 27:1-46; 29:21-27)? Is it surprising to find deception among the patriarchs and matriarchs of the Bible? Why or why not?

_____

_____

_____

_____

4. In the collective memory of Israel, stories of manipulation, deception, and disappointment do not thwart God's plan. Can you think of a time when you have seen God at work in unusual or even self-serving circumstances?

_____

_____

_____

_____

_____

_____

5. The children of Zilpah and Bilhah form four of Israel's twelve tribes. Why can we assume that these two women were never valued in their own right (Gen 33:1-2; 35:22)?

_____

_____

_____

_____

_____

_____

6. Given the culture of the time, do you think Dinah's family was equally concerned about her and their reputation (Gen 34:5-31)? How might Dinah tell the story if given the chance? How might she have experienced God's presence?

_____

_____

_____

_____

_____

7. Israel had provisions in place should a man die and leave his wife widowed. (See Deut 25:5-10.) How does the man's family benefit from this law? How does the widow benefit?

_____

_____

_____

_____

_____

8. In what ways does Tamar show herself to be more "in the right" than Judah (Gen 38:6-30)?

_____

_____

_____

_____

_____

9. In the stories of Israel's beginnings, we cannot help but notice that once God makes a promise, the people involved feel almost compelled to bring it to fruition quickly. They find it hard to trust in God's timing. Does this pattern ring true in your own experience?

_____

_____

_____

_____

_____

10. Continuing the Conversation: Does this essay about Rebekah's power and authority within her family convince you that women may have had more power in ancient Israel than we sometimes assume or imagine? Why or why not?

_____

_____

_____

_____

_____

CLOSING PRAYER

Prayer

[Isaac] took Rebekah as his wife. Isaac loved her and found solace after the death of his mother.

(Gen 24:67)

You have created us, O God, to thrive in relationships with one another. Just as your people in ancient times created families and clans in response to your love, we too ground ourselves in marriage and friendship where we find you present. Today we pray for those in our world who long for comfort and direction, especially . . .

LESSON THREE

Women of Israel's Passover

Begin your personal study and group discussion with a simple and sincere prayer such as:

Prayer

God of Salvation, in these stories of biblical women, may we discover in ourselves a fresh desire to know and love you. Continue to form us as a people of your own.

Read pages 54–63, Lesson Three.

Respond to the questions on pages 64–66, Exploring Lesson Three.

The Closing Prayer on page 66 is for your personal use and may be used at the end of group discussion.

WOMEN OF ISRAEL'S PASSOVER

Scripture excerpts are found in shaded text boxes throughout the lesson. For additional context, you may wish to read all of the following in your Bible: Exodus 1–2; 4:19-26; 15:1-21; 18:1-7; Numbers 12:1-16; 20:1; 27:1-11; 36:1-13; Joshua 17:1-6.

The beginning of the story of Israel's deliverance from enslavement in Egypt is a story of heroic women: midwives, Moses' mother and sister, Pharaoh's daughter and her maids. With the help of these courageous women, the oppression of the Egyptians was broken.

SHIPHRAH AND PUAH

The Midwives

> #### Exodus 1:15-22
>
> [15]The king of Egypt told the Hebrew midwives, one of whom was called Shiphrah and the other Puah, [16]"When you act as midwives for the Hebrew women, look on the birthstool: if it is a boy, kill him; but if it is a girl, she may live." [17]The midwives, however, feared God; they did not do as the king of Egypt had ordered them, but let the boys live. [18]So the king of Egypt summoned the midwives and asked them, "Why have you done this, allowing the boys to live?" [19]The midwives answered Pharaoh, "The Hebrew women are not like the Egyptian women. They are robust and give birth before the midwife arrives." [20]Therefore God dealt well with the midwives; and the people multiplied and grew very numerous. [21]And because the midwives feared God, God built up families for them. [22]Pharaoh then commanded all his people, "Throw into the Nile every boy that is born, but you may let all the girls live."

The story of the midwives interrupts the story of Israel's forced labor in Egypt. The oppressors move from slavery to genocide. The agents in this atrocity are to be the midwives. At the moment of birth, they are to kill each male baby.

Two midwives are singled out to represent the many required to serve Israel's growing population. The two are named, surprising in this story in which many women remain nameless. The name of one is Shiphrah, "fair one," and the other is Puah, probably meaning "girl." It is possible that the women are Egyptian; the phrase "Hebrew midwives" in 1:15 can be translated as "midwives to the Hebrews." This gives greater credibility to Pharaoh's expectation that they will obey his command.

Shiphrah and Puah, however, resist Pharaoh's order. They do not kill Hebrew baby boys. When they are summoned before the Pharaoh, they offer an explanation: "The Hebrew women are not like the Egyptian women. They are robust and give birth before the midwife arrives." The story continues to be surprising. They get away with their civil disobedience and their questionable explanation. These women have found a way to resist oppression. Pharaoh gives up on the women as agents of genocide; instead, he commands all his people to kill Hebrew baby boys.

The Hebrew text states that the women acted so bravely because they feared God. Fear of the Lord is awe and reverence in the recognition of the power and goodness of God. It is wonder in the face of God's overwhelming love. It is trust in the wisdom of God who is more than we can ever imagine. Fear of the Lord is the beginning of wisdom (see Ps 111:10; Prov 9:10) and the distinguishing characteristic of those who are faithful to God's covenant (cf. Deut 6:1-3; Pss 25:14; 34:10).

Because the midwives stand in this right relationship to the living God, they have the courage to honor God's commands. Their reward is the gift of life. God builds up families for them. The implication is that they become part of the covenant people of Israel. They become channels of life for the covenant people. They are the midwives assisting at the birth of Israel.

Who can believe the bravery and creativity of **the midwives** to the Hebrews? In spite of the possibility that they are not Hebrews themselves, their allegiance is first and foremost to God and the ways of God, not to Pharaoh and his ways. Their courage and refusal to participate in bringing about death is a natural consequence of knowing God, the author of life.

The writers of the story of Exodus, centuries after the events unfolded, saw that Shiphrah and Puah embodied the covenant values of mercy, steadfast love, and justice. They demonstrated in their lives what it means to live in covenant. And they remind even modern readers that a basic reverence for God results in good fruit.

MOSES' MOTHER

Exodus 2:1-10

¹Now a man of the house of Levi married a Levite woman, ²and the woman conceived and bore a son. Seeing what a fine child he was, she hid him for three months. ³But when she could no longer hide him, she took a papyrus basket, daubed it with bitumen and pitch, and putting the child in it, placed it among the reeds on the bank of the Nile. ⁴His sister stationed herself at a distance to find out what would happen to him.

⁵Then Pharaoh's daughter came down to bathe at the Nile, while her attendants walked along the bank of the Nile. Noticing the basket among the reeds, she sent her handmaid to fetch it. ⁶On opening it, she looked, and there was a baby boy crying! She was moved with pity for him and said, "It is one of the Hebrews' children." ⁷Then his sister asked Pharaoh's daughter, "Shall I go and summon a Hebrew woman to nurse the child for you?" ⁸Pharaoh's daughter answered her, "Go." So the young woman went and called the child's own mother. ⁹Pharaoh's daughter said to her, "Take this child and nurse him for me, and I will pay your wages." So the woman took the child and nursed him. ¹⁰When the child grew, she brought him to Pharaoh's daughter, and he became her son. She named him Moses; for she said, "I drew him out of the water."

Moses' mother gives birth to the hero of Israel's deliverance and continues the story of resistance to oppression. Although she is nameless in this account, she is named Jochebed in Exodus 6:16-20 and Numbers 26:58-59. These passages come from the later Priestly tradition that commonly gave names to previously unnamed figures who were significant for Israel's story.

After she gives birth, Moses' mother looks at him and sees that he is a "fine" child (*kî tôb* is also translated as "good"). Just so, God looks at the various elements of creation as they are brought forth and says, "How good (*kî tôb*)!" (Gen 1:4, 10, 12, 18, 21, 25). She saves the child from the river by means of a vessel (literally an "ark," *tebah*) daubed with bitumen and pitch. Just so, Noah saved human and animal life from the flood by means of an ark (*tebah*) covered with pitch (Gen 6:14). She endangers the child, turning him over to strangers, and then receives him back with payment (Exod 2:9). Just so, Abraham endangered Sarah and then received her back with added riches (Gen 20:1-18). This mother is described as a source of life for Israel like Noah and Abraham, even like God.

PHARAOH'S DAUGHTER

Pharaoh's daughter is another of the courageous women who are found at the beginning of the Exodus story. The story is simple; the questions are many. This daughter of the man who has commanded that all Hebrew baby boys be thrown into the river sees a baby boy in the river and pities him. She knows the child is Hebrew; she knows why he is in the river. Still she gives the child to a Hebrew woman to nurse and then adopts him as her son. She acts in defiance of her father's order, but her defiance is subtle. She does not confront her father with his injustice. She simply reverses his command. Her action, like that of the midwives, renders the Pharaoh powerless. She has found her own way to break oppression.

Scripture is filled with evidence that God works through those who are considered "outsiders." **Pharaoh's daughter** is one such "outsider" whose story is told in a way that prefigures what God will do on behalf of the enslaved Hebrews. She is so moved with pity upon seeing the endangered child in the basket that she adopts him (Exod 2:1-10). Her actions are quite similar to those of God, who will take note of the enslaved Hebrews, be moved with pity for their plight, and make them his own in a covenant of love (see Exod 3:7-8).

Pharaoh's daughter gives the Hebrew baby an Egyptian name, Moses. The name "Moses" means "to be born." It is found in the names of Thut*mose*, Ah*mose*, and Ra*meses*. Later biblical tradition will give the name a Hebrew

etymology from the Hebrew word, "to draw out." Pharaoh's daughter raises Moses in the Egyptian court. She prepares him for the task God has in mind for him. She trains him in the skills that will enable him to confront and eventually defeat another pharaoh. She is a mother of the exodus.

The biblical text reveals no more. We do not know her name, her motivations, or what happens to her after this scene.

MIRIAM

Sister of Moses

Exodus 2:7-8

[7]Then his sister asked Pharaoh's daughter, "Shall I go and summon a Hebrew woman to nurse the child for you?" [8]Pharaoh's daughter answered her, "Go." So the young woman went and called the child's own mother.

The notice in Exodus 2:7 that the baby Moses has an older sister comes as a surprise. The first verses of this chapter suggest that Moses is the first child of the Levite man and woman. In Exodus 2 the baby's sister is regarded as doubly insignificant: her birth is not mentioned; her name is not given. Yet she, along with the women discussed previously, is a major actor in this scene of deliverance. She is the liaison between Pharaoh's daughter and Moses' mother. This young girl links the women of Egypt and the women of Israel in the act of saving Moses. She has waited bravely, guarding the child; now her action restores the child to his mother.

A sister of Moses is named in the genealogies: Miriam (see Exod 6:20; Num 26:59; 1 Chr 5:29). It is not certain who the nameless sister in Exodus 2 is, but she is typically interpreted as Miriam. The meaning of her name is not clear. It is probably an Egyptian name meaning "beloved." The Greek form of the name is "Mary" and appears frequently in the New Testament, most notably as the name of the mother of Jesus, Mary of Bethany, and Mary Magdalene. The genealogies list the three major leaders of the exodus-wilderness period—Aaron, Moses, and Miriam—as children of one family.

Prophet of Victory

Exodus 15:19-21

¹⁹When Pharaoh's horses and chariots and horsemen entered the sea, the LORD made the waters of the sea flow back upon them, though the Israelites walked on dry land through the midst of the sea. ²⁰Then the prophet Miriam, Aaron's sister, took a tambourine in her hand, while all the women went out after her with tambourines, dancing; ²¹and she responded to them:
Sing to the LORD, for he is gloriously
triumphant;
horse and chariot he has cast into the sea.

The song of Miriam at the crossing of the sea is one of the oldest texts in the Bible. Miriam leads the community in the cultic celebration of victory, setting a precedent for the Holy War tradition. Two centuries later the daughter of Jephthah will come out dancing with tambourines to meet her father after his victory over the Ammonites (Judg 11:34). The heroine Judith will lead the celebration after the defeat of the Assyrians: the women dancing, the men singing hymns (Jdt 15:12–16:2). In the Holy War tradition the victory is due to God's gift, not human power (see Judg 7:1-7; Ps 20:8). The battle is seen as part of a liturgical celebration (see the fall of Jericho in Joshua 6); the victory song led by the women is the conclusion to the liturgy. Miriam is the first to lead such a song; she celebrates God's victory over slavery and death.

Miriam is identified as a prophet (15:20). The function of a prophet is to be a messenger

for God. The prophet has a ministry of imagination, leading the people to understand their present experience and to imagine—and thus be able to achieve—a better future. Miriam's song interprets the exodus experience for the people as a great triumph of God's power, wielded on their behalf.

Challenge to Moses

Numbers 12:1-16

¹Miriam and Aaron spoke against Moses on the pretext of the Cushite woman he had married; for he had in fact married a Cushite woman. ²They complained, "Is it through Moses alone that the LORD has spoken? Has he not spoken through us also?" And the LORD heard this. ³Now the man Moses was very humble, more than anyone else on earth. ⁴So at once the LORD said to Moses and

continue

The Song of Miriam

57

Aaron and Miriam: Come out, you three, to the tent of meeting. And the three of them went. [5]Then the LORD came down in a column of cloud, and standing at the entrance of the tent, called, "Aaron and Miriam." When both came forward, [6]the LORD said: Now listen to my words:

If there are prophets among you,
 in visions I reveal myself to them,
 in dreams I speak to them;
[7]Not so with my servant Moses!
Throughout my house he is worthy of trust:
[8]face to face I speak to him,
 plainly and not in riddles.
The likeness of the LORD he beholds.

Why, then, do you not fear to speak against my servant Moses? [9]And so the LORD's wrath flared against them, and he departed.

[10]Now the cloud withdrew from the tent, and there was Miriam, stricken with a scaly infection, white as snow! When Aaron turned toward Miriam and saw her stricken with snow-white scales, [11]he said to Moses, "Ah, my lord! Please do not charge us with the sin that we have foolishly committed! [12]Do not let her be like the stillborn baby that comes forth from its mother's womb with its flesh half consumed." [13]Then Moses cried to the LORD, "Please, not this! Please, heal her!" [14]But the LORD answered Moses: Suppose her father had spit in her face, would she not bear her shame for seven days? Let her be confined outside the camp for seven days; afterwards she may be brought back. [15]So Miriam was confined outside the camp for seven days, and the people did not start out again until she was brought back.

[16]After that the people set out from Hazeroth and encamped in the wilderness of Paran.

The question of Miriam's role arises in Numbers 12 when she challenges the religious leadership of Moses. Miriam, Aaron, and Moses are certainly the major leaders of the exodus-wilderness period. Is one among them primary? "Is it through Moses alone that the LORD has spoken?" (12:2). Prophetic authority is the real question. Moses' foreign wife is a secondary matter.

God's answer to the question is clear and swift. God may speak through Miriam and Aaron as through other prophets, but Moses is the primary witness. God speaks to him face

More Women of the Old Testament

Women in the Book of Numbers

The book of Numbers includes multiple texts in which women are central. Unfortunately, many of these traditions depict women in unsafe and problematic circumstances, such as being accused of infidelity and experiencing abuse (Num 5). Cozbi, a Midianite woman, is killed by a priest for entering a tent with an Israelite man, an example of hostility towards foreign women because of fears that they would encourage worship of foreign gods (Num 25). Restrictions are imposed on women inheriting property (Num 27, 36), and women are killed or taken as booty during war (Num 31). These texts pose theological challenges, especially in the ways God is depicted as affirming and promoting abuse (see examples in Num 25 and 31). As readers and interpreters, we must sit with the discomfort of such biblical traditions and realize that the motivations of ancient biblical authors might differ from our own contemporary interests and perspectives.

—*Jaime L. Waters*

to face. Any challenges to his leadership, religious or civil, are terribly punished (see Num 16:1–17:15). Miriam is struck immediately with a skin disease. Her condition wrings a plea from Aaron (who seems to escape any punishment!) and a prayer from Moses. But any skin disease, however temporary, requires that the sufferer be confined outside the camp (Lev 13:4-6). Miriam is separated from the community, but the community will not leave without her. They wait for her restoration before continuing their journey.

Miriam's suffering is remembered in the Deuteronomic legislation concerning leprosy (Deut 24:8-9).

Death of Miriam

Numbers 20:1

¹The Israelites, the whole community, arrived in the wilderness of Zin in the first month, and the people stayed at Kadesh. It was here that Miriam died, and here that she was buried.

Numbers 20 indicates that the three desert leaders die in the desert. Miriam's death is reported at the beginning of the chapter, Aaron's death at the end (20:22-29). In between God tells Moses that he will die before the entrance to the land of promise (20:12). Miriam, Moses, and Aaron led Israel out of Egypt and through the desert. It will be the task of the next generation to enter the land.

Miriam is buried at Kadesh, an important sanctuary on Israel's route through the desert. The very name of the place means "sacred." The Israelites encamp there for a long time (Deut 1:46). There the spies make their report on the land (Num 13:25-33); there the people murmur and are told that they will wander in the desert for forty years (Num 14). From there the final journey into the land begins (Num 20:14-22). The notice of Miriam's burial associates her clearly with this significant sanctuary of the desert period.

A Lasting Memory

Micah 6:3-4

³My people, what have I done to you?
  how have I wearied you? Answer me!
⁴I brought you up from the land of Egypt,
  from the place of slavery I ransomed you;
And I sent before you Moses,
  Aaron, and Miriam.

The memory of Miriam continues through the prophetic period. In the eighth century the prophet Micah lists her as one of the great desert leaders, along with Moses and Aaron. She is part of God's gift to the people in the great saving event of the exodus. Micah reports a lawsuit in which God accuses the people of forgetting these wonderful deeds. The people plead guilty and suggest various means of making amends. But God is not satisfied with their offers. God's sentence is more difficult. God demands not that they remove something from their lives, but that they live fully: "to do justice and to love goodness, / and to walk humbly with your God" (Mic 6:8).

Who is Miriam? Some things are certain: She is one of the three great heroes in the desert, equal to Aaron and Moses. She is a cultic leader and prophet, celebrating the divine victory at the sea and mediating God's word to the people. She is respected by the people. They remain at Hazeroth during the seven days of her isolation; their journey will not continue until Miriam is with them. Her story is attached to the sanctuary of Kadesh, a significant site in Israel's desert sojourn.

The image traditionally associated with Miriam is water. As the nameless sister in Exodus 2, she watches the baby in the river. She sings the victory song after the crossing of the sea. She dies at Kadesh where the people complain because they have no water (Num 20:2-5). Her story is as paradoxical as the image of water, which is a symbol of both life and death.

 The ongoing use of **Miriam's name** in both Judaism and Christianity is a clear indication of her important role in Israel's history. The Hebrew name "Miriam" is translated to "Maria" in Latin and "Mary" in English. When Mary, the mother of Jesus, was called by name in her original language, it was most likely *Miriam* or *Maryam*, a lingering tribute to one of the heroes of the exodus.

ZIPPORAH

Betrothal and Marriage

Exodus 2:15-22

¹⁵But Moses fled from Pharaoh and went to the land of Midian. There he sat down by a well. ¹⁶Now the priest of Midian had seven daughters, and they came to draw water and fill the troughs to water their father's flock. ¹⁷But shepherds came and drove them away. So Moses rose up in their defense and watered their flock. ¹⁸When they returned to their father Reuel, he said to them, "How is it you have returned so soon today?" ¹⁹They answered, "An Egyptian delivered us from the shepherds. He even drew water for us and watered the flock!" ²⁰"Where is he?" he asked his daughters. "Why did you leave the man there? Invite him to have something to eat." ²¹Moses agreed to stay with him, and the man gave Moses his daughter Zipporah in marriage. ²²She conceived and bore a son, whom he named Gershom; for he said, "I am a stranger residing in a foreign land."

The story of Moses' betrothal to Zipporah is another betrothal type scene (see chart on p. 32). Several of the elements of the typical scene

are found: a stranger, a well, young women, the drawing of water, an invitation to a meal. One element of the type scene is heightened in this story. Instead of one young woman, there are seven. The number seven often indicates completeness or perfection. Moses is met by a perfect number of young women. One is chosen from this perfection to be his wife. The use of the type scene puts the marriage of Moses and Zipporah in the tradition of the ancestors.

Zipporah, whose name means "swallow," is identified as a daughter of Reuel, a priest of Midian. Moses' genealogy has put him in the family of Levi, a priestly family; his wife also belongs to a priestly family.

Zipporah does not belong to the tradition of barren wives. She bears Moses a son whom Moses names Gershom. The name of the son, from the Hebrew word *ger* which means "sojourner," signifies that Moses is not a permanent resident of Midian. Zipporah's son is the sign of Moses' future return to his people.

Savior of Moses

Exodus 4:19-20, 24-26

¹⁹Then the LORD said to Moses in Midian: Return to Egypt, for all those who sought your life are dead. ²⁰So Moses took his wife and his sons, mounted them on the donkey, and started back to the land of Egypt. Moses took the staff of God with him. . . .

²⁴On the journey, at a place where they spent the night, the LORD came upon Moses and sought to put him to death. ²⁵But Zipporah took a piece of flint and cut off her son's foreskin and, touching his feet, she said, "Surely you are a spouse of blood to me." ²⁶So God let Moses alone. At that time she said, "A spouse of blood," in regard to the circumcision.

The scene in which God would kill Moses is puzzling. It is similar to Genesis 32:23-31 when

God wrestles with Jacob. Both scenes portray God as dangerous and terrifying. God is a night spirit threatening the chosen one as he returns home. In the Genesis story, Jacob holds his own against God and thus wins the name Israel, meaning "the one who contends with God." Moses, on the other hand, is saved by his wife Zipporah. She is the sixth woman in the story of Moses who functions prominently in saving lives: the midwives who save the Israelite baby boys; the mother and sister of Moses, and Pharaoh's daughter, each of whom saves Moses' life.

The act of saving is a circumcision. The story shows Zipporah circumcising her son and touching Moses' penis (the likely meaning behind the euphemistic reference to Moses' "feet") with the bloody foreskin. It is frequently supposed, however, that this story is a veiling of the true event of Zipporah circumcising her husband Moses. In either case Zipporah saves Moses' life, circumcising him physically or symbolically by touching his penis with the blood of their son's circumcision.

There are several reasons why it is imperative that Moses be circumcised. Circumcision is the sign of God's covenant with Abraham and his descendants (Gen 17:10-14). If Moses is not circumcised, he is cut off from God's people (Gen 17:14). Moses, who is called to save the covenant people, must bear the sign of the covenant in his flesh. Circumcision is also a qualification for participating in the Passover celebration, a memorial of Israel's deliverance from Egypt. Moses, who is God's instrument in the deliverance, must himself be circumcised. Finally, although Israel circumcised baby boys on the eighth day after birth (Lev 12:3), circumcision seems originally to have been practiced in the ancient Near East as a rite of initiation, either from boyhood into manhood (e.g., the circumcision of Ishmael at the age of thirteen, Gen 17:25) or as a preparation for marriage (perhaps echoed in Zipporah's reference to Moses as a "spouse of blood").

Zipporah's action is unique and redemptive. Ordinarily circumcision is performed by the father; there is no other biblical story of a woman circumcising anyone. By her action, Zipporah saves Moses' life. She delivers Moses from death, as Moses will deliver the Israelites. She stands between Moses and an angry God, acting as a mediator, just as Moses mediates when God threatens to destroy the people because of the golden calf (Exod 32:1-14).

Zipporah is a significant figure in the life of Israel's great hero, Moses. She is his wife and the mother of his children. She saves his life in a dangerous encounter with God and initiates him into the covenant.

 The **circumcision of Moses' son** occurs just after Moses has objected to God's call not once, but five times (3:11, 13; 4:1, 10, 13). On the way back to Egypt to confront Pharaoh, Zipporah is put in the position to demonstrate to God that they are fully committed. Their son (presumably raised as a Midianite and not accustomed to Israelite ritual), is circumcised by his mother in accord with the command to Abraham (Gen 17:10-12).

CONTINUING THE CONVERSATION

By Jaime L. Waters

Miriam: Prophet and Liturgist

Innovative and subversive women are foundational to the book of Exodus. In Exodus 1–2, women work together and separately to save lives. Shiphrah and Puah subvert a royal order in order to save lives. Likewise, Moses' mother and sister work to protect Moses, along with an Egyptian princess and her servant. According to the biblical narrative, without these women, Moses' life would have ended in infancy, and his pivotal role in the exodus would not have been possible.

It is unclear if Moses' sister in Exodus 2 is Miriam since she is unnamed, but usually it is assumed that she is Miriam since we do not hear of another sister of Moses in Exodus or the books that follow. Miriam is present during and after the exodus from Egypt and during the wilderness experience. The exodus represents a key moment in salvation history. God, hearing the cries of the Israelites, responds by calling Moses to lead the people to a land promised to their ancestor Abraham. Having been saved in multiple ways in his early life, Moses is now called to save God's people.

Miriam's Prophetic Role

After the Israelites successfully escape Egypt, Moses and Miriam reflect on the events in Exodus 15, and Miriam leads the community in a liturgical celebration. Miriam's song and its context in Exodus 15:19-21 contain important information about Miriam. While her song is brief (v. 21),[9] it reveals how her community remembered and reflected on her, especially within the context of the exodus:

[19]When Pharaoh's horses and chariots and horsemen entered the sea, the LORD made the waters of the sea flow back upon them, though the Israelites walked on dry land through the midst of the sea. [20]Then the prophet Miriam, Aaron's sister, took a tambourine in her hand, while all the women went out after her with tambourines, dancing; [21]and she responded to them:

> Sing to the LORD, for he is gloriously triumphant;
> horse and chariot he has cast into the sea.

God's saving action is described, then Miriam is called a prophet (Hebrew *nebiah*, the feminine form of *nabi*, prophet). Prophets in the ancient Israelite context were often viewed as religious intermediaries between people and God. Their ways of prophesying were diverse and could include spoken word and musical performance, as we find in Exodus 15. Identifying Miriam as a prophet is a recognition of her elevated status and leadership role in the community. Wilda C. Gafney, in her book *Daughters of Miriam: Women Prophets in Ancient Israel*, highlights the significance of Miriam within biblical tradition: Miriam is the first woman to be called "prophet," and she embodies prophecy through her word, dance, and music.

Miriam is one of only a few prophetic women in the Old Testament who are named. Other women prophets include Deborah (Judg 4:4), Huldah (2 Kgs 22:14-20; 2 Chr 34:22-28), and No'adiah (Neh 6:14), as well as several women whose names are not recorded, such as the woman prophet in Isaiah (Isa 8:3), women prophets in Ezekiel (Ezek 13:17), and daughters who prophesy (Joel 2:28).

Related to her prophetic role, Miriam is described as using musical instruments and dancing while calling on her community to sing. She is a music minister, a choir conductor, a liturgist. Notice that not only does Miriam lead, but "all the women went out after her." This description offers insight into the ways women participated in liturgy, performing and facilitating worship, especially through music.

Miriam's Punishment

In the book of Numbers, while the Israelites journey through the wilderness after the exodus, Miriam and Aaron question Moses' marriage and whether God speaks exclusively through him (Num 12). This is interpreted as an affront to Moses' prophetic authority. Although Miriam and Aaron both pose questions, and divine wrath is said to be against them because of it, only

Miriam is explicitly punished with diseased skin. This depiction of divine punishment might spark questions about divine justice. The text, however, is primarily concerned with affirming the preeminence of Moses as prophet. Miriam, then, as a prophet, might have been the target for punishment. Aaron, as priest, had different responsibilities and authority that might not have been seen as challenging to Moses, at least not in the same manner as Miriam's prophetic authority.

Ultimately, Miriam recovers, and the Israelites refuse to leave her behind until her skin illness is healed and her period of quarantine ends, showing Miriam's continued significance within the community, even after this incident.

Lesson Three

EXPLORING LESSON THREE

1. Pharaoh was fearful (afraid) of losing power and control, while the midwives feared (stood in awe of) God, which led them to disobey Pharaoh (Exod 1:8-22). Describe a time when your relationship with God has given you the courage to make a difficult decision.

2. Pharaoh saw the Nile River as a means to destroy life (Exod 1:22). How did the mother of Moses see and use the river differently (Exod 2:3)?

3. Pharaoh's daughter defied her father's orders because she was "moved with pity" (Exod 2:6). How does this Egyptian woman embody the qualities of God? (See Ps 72:3; Isa 54:8; 63:9; Mark 1:40-41.)

4. The initial stories of Exodus illustrate women working together to save Moses. Where do you see women collaborating to accomplish good in our world today?

5. a) What is the role of the prophet in Israel? (See Ezek 3:17; Mic 3:8; 2 Pet 1:20-21.)

_____

_____

_____

_____

_____

b) In addition to Miriam (Exod 15:20), who are some of the other women the Bible describes as prophets, and what were their roles? (See Judg 4:4-9; 2 Kgs 22:14-20; Isa 8:1-3; Luke 2:36-38.)

_____

_____

_____

_____

6. While parts of Zipporah's story may strike us as rather strange (Exod 2:16-22; 4:18-26), she is portrayed in a critical moment as a mediator between God and Moses. When has someone been a mediator of God's presence to you?

_____

_____

_____

_____

_____

7. The entire exodus event (from slavery to freedom to covenant) is *the* key event in Israel's history of salvation. What does it tell you that two foreign women—Pharaoh's daughter and Moses' Cushite wife—are instrumental in the life of Moses and therefore in the liberation of the Hebrew people?

_____

_____

_____

_____

_____

_____

8. Continuing the Conversation: When we recall the prophets of ancient Israel, we do not often remember Miriam. Why do you think this is? What have you learned about Miriam in this lesson that will stay with you as you continue your spiritual journey?

_____

_____

_____

_____

_____

9. Continuing the Conversation: The closing essay highlights Miriam's role not only as a prophet but as a liturgist or a "music minister." How does music help us live, proclaim, and understand our relationship with God?

_____

_____

_____

_____

_____

CLOSING PRAYER

Prayer

[Pharaoh's daughter] named him Moses;
for she said, "I drew him out of the water."

(Exod 2:10)

Saving God, in your mercy, send compassionate people into our lives to lift us from drowning in oppression or despair. And then, O Lord, send us to draw others out of the waters that threaten their stability and freedom. We pray for all people who live on the edge of danger, especially . . .

LESSON FOUR

Women of Israel's Early Tribes

Begin your personal study and group discussion with a simple and sincere prayer such as:

Prayer

God of Salvation, in these stories of biblical women, may we discover in ourselves a fresh desire to know and love you. Continue to form us as a people of your own.

Read pages 68–85, Lesson Four.

Respond to the questions on pages 86–88, Exploring Lesson Four.

The Closing Prayer on page 89 is for your personal use and may be used at the end of group discussion.

WOMEN OF ISRAEL'S EARLY TRIBES

Scripture excerpts are found in shaded text boxes throughout the lesson. For additional context, you may wish to read all of the following in your Bible: Joshua 2:1-24; 6:20-25; Judges 4:1–5:31; 11:1-40; 13:1–16:31.

After enduring slavery in Egypt and a time of wilderness wandering, the Israelites enter the promised land. In this tumultuous era of conquest and occupation of the land by Israel's tribes, women serve as protectors, judges, and warriors. They also continue to be recipients of God's word and victims of violence.

RAHAB

The Prostitute

Joshua 2:1-21

¹Then Joshua, son of Nun, secretly sent out two spies from Shittim, saying, "Go, reconnoiter the land and Jericho." When the two reached Jericho, they went into the house of a prostitute named Rahab, where they lodged. ²But a report was brought to the king of Jericho: "Some men came here last night, Israelites, to spy out the land." ³So the king of Jericho sent Rahab the order, "Bring out the men who have come to you and entered your house, for they have come to spy out the entire land." ⁴The woman had taken the two men and hidden them, so she said, "True, the men you speak of came to me, but I did not know where they came from. ⁵At dark, when it was time to close the gate, they left, and I do not know where they went. You will have to pursue them quickly to overtake them." ⁶Now, she had led them to the roof, and hidden them among her stalks of flax spread out there. ⁷But the pursuers set out along the way to the fords of the Jordan. As soon as they had left to pursue them, the gate was shut.

⁸Before the spies lay down, Rahab went up to them on the roof ⁹and said: "I know that the LORD has given you the land, that a dread of you has come upon us, and that all the inhabitants of the land tremble with fear because of you. ¹⁰For we have heard how the LORD dried up the waters of the Red Sea before you when you came out of Egypt, and what you did to Sihon and Og, the two kings of the Amorites beyond the Jordan, whom you destroyed under the ban. ¹¹We heard, and our hearts melted within us; everyone is utterly dispirited because of you, since the LORD, your God, is God in heaven above and on earth below. ¹²Now then, swear to me by the LORD that, since I am showing kindness to you, you in turn will show kindness to my family. Give me a reliable sign ¹³that you will allow my father and mother, brothers and sisters, and my whole family to live, and that you will deliver us from death." ¹⁴"We pledge our lives for yours," they answered her. "If you do not betray our mission, we will be faithful in showing kindness to you when the LORD gives us the land."

¹⁵Then she let them down through the window with a rope; for she lived in a house built into the city wall. ¹⁶"Go up into the hill country," she said, "that your pursuers may not come upon you. Hide there for three days, until they return; then you may go on your way." ¹⁷They answered her, "We are free of this oath that you made us take, unless,

¹⁸when we come into the land, you tie this scarlet cord in the window through which you are letting us down. Gather your father and mother, your brothers, and all your family into your house. ¹⁹Should any of them pass outside the doors of your house, their blood will be on their own heads, and we will be guiltless. But if anyone in your house is harmed, their blood will be on our heads. ²⁰If, however, you betray our mission, we will be free of the oath you have made us take." ²¹"Let it be as you say," she replied, and sent them away. When they were gone, she tied the scarlet cord in the window.

Just as women were instrumental in the exodus of Israel from Egypt, so a woman is significant in Israel's entrance into the promised land. The spies sent by Joshua to reconnoiter the land stay in the house of a woman named Rahab, who is identified as a prostitute. Her house, or inn, is built into the city wall. Her family also lives in the city—father, mother, brothers, and so on (6:23). No husband or children are mentioned; she is a working woman, responsible for her own support.

Later tradition modified the image of Rahab. Josephus, a first-century Jewish historian, calls her simply an innkeeper (Ant., 5.1 para 2). It is not surprising that the two professions of prostitute and innkeeper are mingled; prejudice likely assumed that a woman who kept a hotel must be a prostitute or running a house of prostitution.

News collects at an inn; strangers are less conspicuous there. Perhaps this is why the spies choose to stay with Rahab who herself has heard the news about the Israelites encamped across the Jordan. She not only knows of the exodus and the victories over local kings; she knows that God has given them the land. Her speech (2:9-13) is a testimony of faith in the God of Israel.

Rahab's faith is manifested not only in words, but also in actions. She shows *hesed*, faithful covenant love ("kindness," NABRE),

to the spies (2:12). She hides them and sends their pursuers on a wild goose chase. Having shown *hesed* to the spies, she requests *hesed* in return. She asks that they spare her family in the battle for Jericho, and the men pledge to do so. This Canaanite woman represents the many Canaanites who will join Israel and become part of the covenant people. The account's repetition of the covenant virtues—*hesed* and *emeth* (love/kindness and fidelity)—signifies Rahab's entrance into the covenant (2:12-14; cf. 6:25).

In the Midst of Israel

Joshua 6:20-25

²⁰As the horns blew, the people began to shout. When they heard the sound of the horn, they raised a tremendous shout. The wall collapsed, and the people attacked the city straight ahead and took it. ²¹They observed the ban by putting to the sword all living creatures in the city: men and women, young and old, as well as oxen, sheep and donkeys.

²²To the two men who had spied out the land, Joshua said, "Go into the prostitute's house and bring out the woman with all her family, as you swore to her you would do." ²³The spies entered and brought out Rahab, with her father, mother, brothers, and all her family; her entire family they led forth and placed outside the camp of Israel. ²⁴The city itself they burned with all that was in it; but the silver, gold, and articles of bronze and iron they placed in the treasury of the house of the LORD. ²⁵Because Rahab the prostitute had hidden the messengers whom Joshua had sent to reconnoiter Jericho, Joshua let her live, along with her father's house and all her family, who dwell in the midst of Israel to this day.

Jericho is the first city in the land taken by the entering Israelites. In taking the city they carry out the customs of Holy War. One such custom is the *herem*, or "ban." There are no prisoners captured; there is no plunder taken. No one is to get rich from war. Therefore all living things are killed, all material things destroyed. It is a harsh custom. There are to be no exceptions.

The threat to Rahab and her family is obvious. The spies, however, are faithful to their word. The command is given to put everything in the city under the ban except Rahab and her family (6:17). Joshua sends the spies themselves to fetch her and her family.

Rahab is an independent businesswoman who deceives her king in order to protect Israel. She is a courageous woman who entrusts her future and that of her family to an unknown people and an unknown God. She has heard of this God, however. She already practices covenant virtues and expects them in return. God answers her trust with generous love. She and her family "dwell in the midst of Israel to this day," a part of God's covenant people.

Rahab is named in the letter to the Hebrews as an example of faith: "By faith Rahab the harlot did not perish with the disobedient, for she had received the spies in peace" (Heb 11:31). The letter of James singles her out along with Abraham as an example of someone who demonstrates faith by good works: "[W]as not Rahab the harlot also justified by works when she welcomed the messengers and sent them out by a different route?" (Jas 2:25). Rahab is one of the five women listed in Matthew's genealogy of Jesus (Matt 1:5). She is named as the mother of Boaz who will marry Ruth (Lesson Five). Ruth, another foreign woman who practices the covenant virtue of *hesed* and becomes a mother in Israel, will be the great-grandmother of David.

DEBORAH AND JAEL

Deborah: The Judge, Prophet, and Military Leader

Judges 4:1-16

[1]The Israelites again did what was evil in the sight of the LORD. . . . [2]So the LORD sold them into the power of the Canaanite king, Jabin, who reigned in Hazor. The general of his army was Sisera, who lived in Harosheth-ha-goiim. [3]But the Israelites cried out to the LORD; for with his nine hundred iron chariots Jabin harshly oppressed the Israelites for twenty years.

[4]At that time the prophet Deborah, wife of Lappidoth, was judging Israel. [5]She used to sit under Deborah's palm tree, between Ramah and Bethel in the mountain region of Ephraim, where the Israelites came up to her for judgment. [6]She had Barak, son of Abinoam, summoned from Kedesh of Naphtali. She said to him, "This is what the LORD, the God of Israel, commands: Go, march against Mount Tabor, and take with you ten thousand men from Naphtali and Zebulun. [7]I will draw Sisera, the general of Jabin's army, out to you at the Wadi Kishon, together with his chariots and troops, and I will deliver them into your power." [8]But Barak answered her, "If you come with me, I will go; if you do not come with me, I will not go." [9]"I will certainly go with you," she replied, "but you will not gain glory for the expedition on which you are setting out, for it is

The Song of Deborah

into a woman's power that the LORD is going to sell Sisera." So Deborah arose and went with Barak and journeyed with him to Kedesh.

¹⁰Barak summoned Zebulun and Naphtali to Kedesh, and ten thousand men followed him. Deborah also went up with him. ¹¹Now Heber the Kenite had detached himself from Cain, the descendants of Hobab, Moses' father-in-law, and had pitched his tent by the terebinth of Zaanannim, which was near Kedesh.

¹²It was reported to Sisera that Barak, son of Abinoam, had gone up to Mount Tabor. ¹³So Sisera called out all nine hundred of his iron chariots and all his forces from Harosheth-ha-goiim to the Wadi Kishon. ¹⁴Deborah then said to Barak, "Up! This is the day on which the LORD has delivered Sisera into your power. The LORD marches before you." So Barak went down Mount Tabor, followed by his ten thousand men. ¹⁵And the LORD threw Sisera and all his chariots and forces into a panic before Barak. Sisera himself dismounted from his chariot and fled on foot, ¹⁶but Barak pursued the chariots and the army as far as Harosheth-ha-goiim. The entire army of Sisera fell beneath the sword, not even one man surviving.

The book of Judges is a collection of hero stories from Israel's frontier period. There are twelve stories, linked by the same pattern: (1) Israel offends God; (2) God is angry and gives (literally, sells) them to their enemies; (3) the Israelites cry out; (4) God sends someone called a judge to save them, and (5) the land has rest for a certain number of years. When the judge dies, the pattern repeats.

Deborah is one of the twelve judge-heroes. Most of the judges were military heroes; a few were assassins. In the book of Judges, only Deborah acts as a "judge" in the modern sense, settling disputes. She is also called a prophet (4:4), one who speaks the word of God. Her name is Deborah, which means "honeybee" or "leader." She is called the wife of Lappidoth, which may be translated as "the woman of torches." She sits under "Deborah's palm tree" and exercises judgment. Is the tree named

for her? Or is the tree named for Rebekah's beloved nurse, who was buried under the "oak of weeping" (see Gen 35:8)?

As the deadly cycle of sin and suffering begins, Deborah summons a man, Barak, whose name means "lightning," to function as the military leader. Deborah outlines the strategy for the battle (4:6-7) and determines the moment of attack (4:14). Deborah, the prophet, announces the word of the Lord; Barak, the general, follows her command. Barak is well aware that Deborah holds the power: he refuses to take the commission unless she goes with him. She also is aware of her power: she informs him that the glory of victory will not fall to him but to a woman (4:8-9).

Judges 5:1-23

¹On that day Deborah sang this song—and
    Barak, son of Abinoam:
²When uprising broke out in Israel,
    when the people rallied for duty—bless
        the LORD!
³Hear, O kings! Give ear, O princes!
    I will sing, I will sing to the LORD,
    I will make music to the LORD, the God
        of Israel.
⁴LORD, when you went out from Seir,
    when you marched from the plains of
        Edom,
The earth shook, the heavens poured,
    the clouds poured rain,
⁵The mountains streamed,
    before the LORD, the One of Sinai,
    before the LORD, the God of Israel.
⁶In the days of Shamgar, son of Anath,
    in the days of Jael, caravans ceased:
Those who traveled the roads
    now traveled by roundabout paths.
⁷Gone was freedom beyond the walls,
    gone indeed from Israel.
When I, Deborah, arose,
    when I arose, a mother in Israel.

continue

⁸New gods were their choice;
  then war was at the gates.
No shield was to be found, no spear,
  among forty thousand in Israel!
⁹My heart is with the leaders of Israel,
  with the dedicated ones of the people—
    bless the LORD;
¹⁰Those who ride on white donkeys,
  seated on saddle rugs,
  and those who travel the road,
Sing of them
  ¹¹to the sounds of musicians at the wells.
There they recount the just deeds of the
    LORD,
  his just deeds bringing freedom to Israel.
¹²Awake, awake, Deborah!
  Awake, awake, strike up a song!
Arise, Barak!
  Take captive your captors, son of
    Abinoam!
¹³Then down went Israel against the mighty,
  the army of the LORD went down for him
    against the warriors.
¹⁴From Ephraim, their base in the valley;
  behind you, Benjamin, among your
    troops.
From Machir came down commanders,
  from Zebulun wielders of the marshal's
    staff.
¹⁵The princes of Issachar were with Deborah,
  Issachar, faithful to Barak;
  in the valley they followed at his heels.
Among the clans of Reuben
  great were the searchings of heart!
¹⁶Why did you stay beside your hearths
  listening to the lowing of the herds?
Among the clans of Reuben
  great were the searchings of heart!
¹⁷Gilead stayed beyond the Jordan;
  Why did Dan spend his time in ships?
Asher remained along the shore,
  he stayed in his havens.
¹⁸Zebulun was a people who defied death,
  Naphtali, too, on the open heights!
¹⁹The kings came and fought;
  then they fought, those kings of Canaan,

At Taanach by the waters of Megiddo;
  no spoil of silver did they take.
²⁰From the heavens the stars fought;
  from their courses they fought against
    Sisera.
²¹The Wadi Kishon swept them away;
  the wadi overwhelmed them, the Wadi
    Kishon.
Trample down the strong!
²²Then the hoofs of the horses hammered,
  the galloping, galloping of steeds.
²³"Curse Meroz," says the messenger of the
    LORD,
  "curse, curse its inhabitants!
For they did not come when the LORD
    helped,
  the help of the LORD against the
    warriors."

Judges 5 is the song of Deborah, the poetic retelling of the story of victory at the Wadi Kishon. It is a rule of thumb that when a story appears twice—once in prose and once in poetry—the poetic version is older. The song of Deborah is thus the older version of the story, one of the oldest texts in the Bible itself.

 Several **songs** appear in Scripture as poetic ways of remembering, telling, and assigning meaning to an important event. While a narrative version of these events can be memorable, sung or poetic recitals became part of the emerging liturgy of God's people and are often referred to as **canticles**. (For additional examples, see the song of Moses in Exod 15:1-21; the song of the three young men in Dan 3:52-90; the song of Mary, the *Magnificat*, in Luke 1:46-55; the song of Zechariah in Luke 1:67-79; and the song of Simeon in Luke 2:29-32.)

In the song, Deborah is clearly presented as the leader. She is the one who rose up, "a mother in Israel," to deliver her people (5:7).

Her heart went with the warriors; they were with her as well as Barak (5:9, 15). The two of them take up their respective roles in the Holy War drama: Barak leads the battle, Deborah leads the victory song (5:12; cf. Exod 15).

In the period of the judges (ca. 1250 BCE) the Israelites had no central leader and no capital city. Their form of government can be compared to the government of the United States under the Articles of Confederation (1781–1789), when the rights of the states were primary. In Israel the rights of the tribes were primary. The twelve tribes were united by the covenant, symbolized by the ark of the covenant. There was no central sanctuary. The ark of the covenant moved from shrine to shrine. Wherever it was, there was Israel's official place of prayer and center of power.

The twelve judges are tribal leaders, not leaders of all Israel. A complaint continually made by them is that only a few neighboring tribes can be summoned to help in any crisis. The same complaint is registered in Deborah's song (5:14-18). Deborah, however, manages to muster six tribes—Ephraim, Benjamin, Manasseh, Zebulun, Issachar, and Naphtali—the largest number gathered by any of the twelve judges. It is a testimony to the power of her leadership. The combined forces win a great victory "and the land was at rest for forty years" (5:31).

Jael: The Assassin

Judges 4:17-24

[17]Sisera fled on foot to the tent of Jael, wife of Heber the Kenite, for there was peace between Jabin, king of Hazor, and the family of Heber the Kenite. [18]Jael went out to meet Sisera and said to him, "Turn aside, my lord, turn aside with me; do not be afraid." So he went into her tent, and she covered him with a rug. [19]He said to her, "Please give me a little water to drink. I am thirsty." So she opened a skin of milk, gave him a drink, and then covered him. [20]"Stand at the entrance of the tent," he said to her. "If anyone comes and asks, 'Is there someone here?' say, 'No!'" [21]Jael, wife of Heber, got a tent peg and took a mallet in her hand. When Sisera was in a deep sleep from exhaustion, she approached him stealthily and drove the peg through his temple and down into the ground, and he died. [22]Then when Barak came in pursuit of Sisera, Jael went out to meet him and said to him, "Come, I will show you the man you are looking for." So he went in with her, and there lay Sisera dead, with the tent peg through his temple.

[23]Thus on that day God humbled the Canaanite king, Jabin, before the Israelites; [24]their power weighed ever more heavily on him, until at length they finished off the Canaanite king, Jabin.

 The **stories of the judges** are told in a way that reinforces a common belief at the time: the people are punished if they sin but rescued if they repent. The pattern of these stories is as follows:

Pattern	Othniel	Ehud	Deborah	Gideon	Jephthah
The people sin.	3:7	3:12	4:1	6:1	10:6
The Lord is "angry" and allows their defeat.	3:8	3:12-13	4:2	6:1	10:7
The people cry out.	3:9	3:15	4:3	6:7	10:10
The Lord sends a judge to deliver them.	3:9	3:15	(cf. 4:4)	(cf. 6:14)	(cf. 11:29)
There is peace until the judge dies.	3:11	3:30	5:31	8:28	----

Deborah predicted that God would give the glory of victory to a woman (4:9). The woman is not Deborah herself but Jael. Women rarely appear alone in the Bible. For good or for ill their stories are woven together. So, too, Deborah and Jael. The victory belongs to them both.

Jael, whose name means "mountain goat," is introduced as the "wife of Heber the Kenite." The Kenites were a group of metalworking nomads, identified as relatives of Moses (4:11; cf. Num 10:29). The family of Heber has made peace with the Canaanite king Jabin. Sisera, therefore, could expect to be protected in Heber's tent.

Jael takes the initiative in the encounter with Sisera. She goes out to meet him, invites him into the tent, and takes very good care of him! When he asks for water, she gives milk. She covers him twice (4:18, 19). Apparently her solicitude lulls Sisera into trusting her. He appoints her as sentinel to guard the entrance of the tent while he sleeps. Then "Jael, wife of Heber, got a tent peg" and killed Sisera. The murder is particularly gruesome. She kills him with the tent peg, driving it into his temple.

When Barak arrives, Jael greets him exactly as she greeted Sisera and brings him into her tent to see the results of her action. He is too late. She has done his work for him. Jael has destroyed the enemy of his people, a people not her own.

Judges 5:24-31

24Most blessed of women is Jael,
   the wife of Heber the Kenite,
   blessed among tent-dwelling women!
25He asked for water, she gave him milk,
   in a princely bowl she brought him curds.
26With her hand she reached for the peg,
   with her right hand, the workman's
      hammer.
She hammered Sisera, crushed his head;
   she smashed, pierced his temple.
27At her feet he sank down, fell, lay still;
   down at her feet he sank and fell;

Jael and Sisera

where he sank down, there he fell, slain.
²⁸From the window she looked down,
   the mother of Sisera peered through the
      lattice:
"Why is his chariot so long in coming?
   why are the hoofbeats of his chariots
      delayed?"
²⁹The wisest of her princesses answers her;
   she even replies to herself,
³⁰"They must be dividing the spoil they took:
   a slave woman or two for each man,
Spoil of dyed cloth for Sisera,
   spoil of ornate dyed cloth,
   a pair of ornate dyed cloths for my neck
      in the spoil."
³¹So perish all your enemies, O LORD!
   But may those who love you be like the
      sun rising in its might!

The second half of Deborah's song is devoted to Jael's deed. She is introduced at the beginning of the song: "In the days of Shamgar, son of Anath, / in the days of Jael, caravans ceased" (5:6). The stories of Shamgar (Judg 3:31) and Jael surround the story of Deborah.

The story of Jael's action begins with a beatitude: "Most blessed of women is Jael" (5:24). Only two other biblical women are hailed as "blessed among women": Judith (Jdt 13:18) and Mary, the mother of Jesus (Luke 1:42). All three are instrumental in the salvation of the people and in the destruction of the people's enemy.

The following verses describe Sisera's death with grisly cheer. Jael "smashed" and "pierced." Sisera "sank down, fell, lay still," "sank and fell," "sank down," and "fell, slain." There is no doubt of Sisera's fate; there is no doubt of the poet's loyalty. Jael is a hero! The song of Deborah tells her story with obvious delight.

The vocabulary of verse 27 is suggestive of other realities surrounding war and the relationship between men and women. Rape is often a consequence of war for women. Sisera "sinks down" (kneels/crouches), "falls," and lies "at her feet" (or between her legs). The Hebrew words, especially taken together, have a strong sexual connotation. The description is an allusion to rape; however, in this incident the man is the victim. Sisera's fall between Jael's legs is his undoing.

The vocabulary of this verse also suggests birth. In giving birth a woman crouches (cf. 1 Sam 4:19; Job 39:3); a child falls from between her legs. She gives the child milk; she covers it (cf. Judg 4:19; 5:25). Jael acts as a mother to Sisera, giving him milk and covering him for sleep. Unlike a child being born, however, Sisera is not entering life but leaving it. The interweaving of mother imagery is striking. Deborah is "a mother in Israel" (5:7). Jael "mothers" Sisera, while his own mother awaits his return (5:28).

The violence of Jael's actions offends many of us, and some might consider it doubly offensive because Jael is a woman. What motivated this woman, a Kenite whose husband was allied with Jabin, to kill his army general? There may be two reasons. First, if Sisera is fleeing in defeat,

 Three women in Scripture are called "**blessed among women.**" All three are credited with saving the people from a mortal enemy.

Judges 4:21	Jael	Assassinates Sisera, general of Hazor, and thus saves the people from the Canaanites
Judith 13:18	Judith	Assassinates Holofernes, Nebuchadnezzar's general, and thus saves the people from the Assyrians
Luke 1:42	Mary	Gives birth to Jesus, the Son of God, who will save the people from sin and death

the Israelite army cannot be far behind. A grisly fate awaits a woman who shelters an enemy general in her tent, as she could be vulnerable to sexual assault (alluded to in Judg 5:30). Second, from the standpoint of the book of Judges, the heroes are those who deliver the people from the enemy—usually by military action, sometimes by assassination (see Ehud in Judg 3:12-30). Jael is praised as a hero by these standards.

JEPHTHAH'S DAUGHTER

Judges 11:29-40

²⁹The spirit of the LORD came upon Jephthah. He passed through Gilead and Manasseh, and through Mizpah of Gilead as well, and from Mizpah of Gilead he crossed over against the Ammonites. ³⁰Jephthah made a vow to the LORD. "If you deliver the Ammonites into my power," he said, ³¹"whoever comes out of the doors of my house to meet me when I return from the Ammonites in peace shall belong to the LORD. I shall offer him up as a burnt offering."

³²Jephthah then crossed over against the Ammonites to fight against them, and the LORD delivered them into his power. ³³He inflicted a very severe defeat on them from Aroer to the approach of Minnith—twenty cities in all—and as far as Abel-keramin. So the Ammonites were brought into subjection by the Israelites. ³⁴When Jephthah returned to his house in Mizpah, it was his daughter who came out to meet him, with tambourine-playing and dancing. She was his only child: he had neither son nor daughter besides her. ³⁵When he saw her, he tore his garments and said, "Ah, my daughter! You have struck me down and brought calamity upon me. For I have made a vow to the LORD and I cannot take it back." ³⁶"Father," she replied, "you have made a vow to the LORD. Do with me as you have vowed, because the LORD has taken vengeance for you against your enemies the Ammonites." ³⁷Then she said to her father, "Let me have this favor. Do nothing for two months, that I and my companions may go wander in the mountains to weep for my virginity." ³⁸"Go," he replied, and sent her away for two months. So she departed with her companions and wept for her virginity in the mountains. ³⁹At the end of the two months she returned to her father, and he did to her as he had vowed. She had not had relations with any man.

It became a custom in Israel ⁴⁰for Israelite women to go yearly to mourn the daughter of Jephthah the Gileadite for four days of the year.

Jephthah is another judge-hero, called to deliver his people from a threatening enemy. Like most of the other judges, he performs this task through military victory. His story is remembered, however, not so much because of his own exploits, but because of his daughter.

Two things happen as Jephthah is going out to battle. First of all, the spirit of the Lord comes upon him. This is a common phrase in the book of Judges (3:10; 11:29; 14:6, 19; 15:14; cf. 6:34; 13:25). It signifies God's power on the chosen hero; his victory will be God's. But apparently this is not enough for Jephthah. Secondly, he makes a vow, promising God a sacrifice if God will give him the victory. The victim of the sacrifice will be the first living thing—human or animal—who meets him after the victory.

Jephthah's vow presents several problems. It seems he does not trust God and finds it necessary to bargain or bribe. Is he insecure because of his tenuous position in the family (11:1-3)? It also appears that he is willing to make a human sacrifice. Human sacrifice is generally criticized and condemned in the Old Testament, although Judges 11 is a notable exception. Abraham is stopped from sacrificing his son (Gen 22:12-13). Various kings are severely criticized for sacrificing children (2 Kgs 16:3; 21:6; 2 Chr 28:3; 33:6). The law forbids human sacrifice (Lev 18:21; 20:2-5; Deut 12:31). The other nations are scorned because they practice it (2 Kgs 17:31; Ps 106:34-38). The prophets rail against it (Jer 7:31; 19:5; Ezek

16:20-21; 20:31). But Jephthah's vow allows for, even suggests, a human sacrifice.

A third dilemma is presented by the vow. Ancient peoples, including Israel, had a great respect for the power of the spoken word. A word once spoken took on its own power. Isaac's blessing of Jacob, once spoken, cannot be taken back (Gen 27:37). The content of curses was often disguised, for fear that their spoken words might rebound on the speaker (e.g., Ruth 1:17; 1 Sam 3:17; 14:44). Jephthah has spoken his vow; it cannot be taken back.

The designated victim of the sacrifice is his daughter, his only child. She emerges from the house first, carrying out the woman's role in victory. Like Miriam she leads the celebration, playing the tambourines and dancing (Exod 15:20; cf. 1 Sam 18:6; Jdt 15:12–16:2). But her celebration is her death sentence. Jephthah's exclamation upon seeing her is ironic: "Ah, my daughter! *You* have struck me down and brought calamity upon me" (11:35, emphasis mine). The disaster is her own fault; the blame for her death is laid upon her. Her father—bound by his vow—uses it to claim innocence.

The daughter surrenders to her father's vow. She asks only one favor, to go off with her companions to mourn her virginity. The woman's virginity signals that she will die childless. Her legacy will not continue by children. However, the woman's life and death impact other women's lives, thus creating a new legacy for her. Her death becomes the occasion for Israelite women to mourn her for four days every year. She lives on in their memory.

Jephthah's daughter is remembered by the women but forgotten in the rest of the biblical story. Her father Jephthah is held up by Samuel as an example of those God sent to deliver Israel (1 Sam 12:11). He is held up by the author of the letter to the Hebrews as an example of faith and righteousness (Heb 11:32-33). His daughter is not mentioned again. But is Jephthah really a hero? Can we bear to consider him as such?

Should Jephthah's daughter have surrendered to her horrible death? That question has engaged commentators, especially in this cen-tury. Some see her as a model of obedience; many assume that she had no choice. But she has also been criticized for not defying such a foolish vow. Recently it has also been suggested that the real point of her story is the women's yearly celebration mentioned in verse 40. Her story may belong to a rite of passage, a story of death to childhood at the beginning of puberty.

Jephthah's daughter remains a tragic figure in biblical literature. She is sacrificed for her father's victory, her father's glory, her father's religion. Her father will not back down on his vow. Neither, it seems, will God. This time there is no ram in the thicket, no change of plan (cf. Gen 22:13; 1 Sam 14:24-26, 43-45). Jephthah's daughter dies as a burnt offering, the victim of a vow. Israel's deliverance is bought at the price of her life.

SAMSON'S MOTHER

Judges 13:1-25

¹The Israelites again did what was evil in the sight of the LORD, who therefore delivered them into the power of the Philistines for forty years.

²There was a certain man from Zorah, of the clan of the Danites, whose name was Manoah. His wife was barren and had borne no children. ³An angel of the LORD appeared to the woman and said to her: Though you are barren and have had no children, you will conceive and bear a son. ⁴Now, then, be careful to drink no wine or beer and to eat nothing unclean, ⁵for you will conceive and bear a son. No razor shall touch his head, for the boy is to be a nazirite for God from the womb. It is he who will begin to save Israel from the power of the Philistines.

⁶The woman went and told her husband, "A man of God came to me; he had the appearance of an angel of God, fearsome indeed. I did not ask him where he came from, nor did he tell me his name. ⁷But he said to me, 'You will conceive and

continue

bear a son. So drink no wine or beer, and eat nothing unclean. For the boy shall be a nazirite for God from the womb, until the day of his death.'" [8]Manoah then prayed to the LORD. "Please, my Lord," he said, "may the man of God whom you sent return to us to teach us what to do for the boy who is to be born."

[9]God heard the prayer of Manoah, and the angel of God came again to the woman as she was sitting in the field; but her husband Manoah was not with her. [10]The woman ran quickly and told her husband. "The man who came to me the other day has appeared to me," she said to him; [11]so Manoah got up and followed his wife. When he reached the man, he said to him, "Are you the one who spoke to my wife?" I am, he answered. [12]Then Manoah asked, "Now, when what you say comes true, what rules must the boy follow? What must he do?" [13]The angel of the LORD answered Manoah: Your wife must be careful about all the things of which I spoke to her. [14]She must not eat anything that comes from the vine, she must not drink wine or beer, and she must not eat anything unclean. Let her observe all that I have commanded her. [15]Then Manoah said to the angel of the LORD, "Permit us to detain you, so that we may prepare a young goat for you." [16]But the angel of the LORD answered Manoah: Though you detained me, I would not eat your food. But if you want to prepare a burnt offering, then offer it up to the LORD. For Manoah did not know that he was the angel of the LORD. [17]Then Manoah said to the angel of the LORD, "What is your name, that we may honor you when your words come true?" [18]The angel of the LORD answered him: Why do you ask my name? It is wondrous. [19]Then Manoah took a young goat with a grain offering and offered it on the rock to the LORD, who works wonders. While Manoah and his wife were looking on, [20]as the flame rose to the heavens from the altar, the angel of the LORD ascended in the flame of the altar. When Manoah and his wife saw this, they fell on their faces to the ground; [21]but the angel of the LORD was seen no more by Manoah and his wife. Then Manoah, realizing that it was the angel of the LORD, [22]said to his wife, "We will certainly die, for we have seen God." [23]But his wife said to him, "If the LORD had meant to kill us, he would not have accepted a burnt offering and grain offering from our hands! Nor would he have let us see all this, or hear what we have heard."

[24]The woman bore a son and named him Samson, and when the boy grew up the LORD blessed him. [25]The spirit of the LORD came upon him for the first time in Mahaneh-dan, between Zorah and Eshtaol.

The book of Judges borrows many patterns and themes from earlier narratives. Within the story of Samson, which is based on the common pattern of judge stories, there are other smaller forms. The way the forms are used reveals the meaning in the story. One such form is an extended announcement of birth form. Within this chapter we also find the barren wife theme, a description of the nazirite vow, and the encounter between human beings and the angel of the Lord. Throughout the chapter, the wife of Manoah is a central figure.

The use of the announcement of birth form (see p. 18) signals the importance of this child. God will bless the Israelites through him and deliver them from their enemies. The announcement of birth begins with the appearance of the angel of the Lord to the wife of Manoah. The second element of the form, however, is missing: she expresses no fear. In fact, the only expression of fear in the whole chapter comes from her husband when he finally realizes that this is indeed an angel of the Lord (13:21-22). The form continues with the third element, the message. The angel tells Manoah's wife that she will bear a son and reveals to her the son's future mission. There is no mention of the son's name.

At this point the form is stretched. The conversation between the angel and the woman ends, and she goes to report the event to Manoah. He asks for a second appearance which God grants. The message is repeated, and Manoah suggests a sacrifice. The only hint of an objection (the fourth element of the form) is Manoah's constant questioning that ends with a request for the angel's name. The request is refused but the sacrifice is accepted. The angel ascends within the sacrificial flame (perhaps a sign, which is the sixth element) and Manoah is sure they will die. The reassurance (fifth element) comes not from the angel but from the woman: If the Lord were going to kill us, she reasons, our sacrifice would not have been accepted, and we would not have been given this message. The announcement of birth is fulfilled: The woman bears a son and names him Samson. The spirit of the Lord comes upon him (13:25; cf. 14:6, 19; 15:14).

The variation in the form alerts us to the presence of a deeper message. The effect of the subtle changes is to emphasize the importance of the woman. We expect someone to object to the impending birth, but this woman does not object. The second appearance of the angel, this time to the woman with her husband, provides the opportunity for an objection from her husband. We also expect a reassurance. Ordinarily it would come from the angel, but in this story, it comes from the woman. These varia-

tions make clear the faith of this extraordinary woman and her willingness to be a channel of God's care for the people. In the story of Samson, no other character shows such faith and obedience to God.

Appearances of angels often strike terror in human beings. There is a tradition that no human being can see the face of God (even reflected on the face of an angel) and live. Because of this tradition, Manoah thinks they will die. However, while there are no stories of anyone dying from such a vision, there are many stories of amazement that life continues after such an event (e.g., Hagar in Gen 16:13; Jacob in Gen 32:31; and the Sinai community in Exod 20:19). Manoah does not understand the messenger of God, but his wife does.

It is also the woman who is entrusted with the child's nazirite vow (13:4-5, 7, 13-14). A nazirite vow is a special consecration to God. The signs of this consecration are abstaining from strong drink, avoiding all contact with dead bodies, and not cutting the hair (see Num 6:2-8). Samuel (1 Sam 1:11, 22-28) and John the Baptist (Luke 1:13-15) were also nazirites for life, and Paul made a temporary nazirite vow (Acts 18:18). This vow will be very important in the life of Samson (see Judg 16). Because it is a consecration from the womb, Samson's mother keeps the vow for him as long as she carries him. She is more faithful to it than Samson will be. She is the one to whom the instructions for the vow are given. She repeats them to her husband as the angel will later do. She is responsible for the vow.

Manoah's wife is the primary recipient of the announcement of birth, just as Hagar was (Gen 16:7-16). Even in the second appearance, requested by her husband, the angel appears to her first. She is an example of faith: she listens to the word of God mediated through the angel; she builds her life around that word. She is another barren wife in the tradition of Sarah, Rebekah, and Rachel. It is she who recognizes the angel (13:6) and she who understands the significance of the message. They will not die but live to carry out God's plan. It is through this nameless woman that God chooses to work.

SAMSON'S WIFE

Judges 14:1-4

¹Samson went down to Timnah where he saw one of the Philistine women. ²On his return he told his father and mother, "I saw in Timnah a woman, a Philistine. Get her for me as a wife." ³His father and mother said to him, "Is there no woman among your kinsfolk or among all your people, that you must go and take a woman from the uncircumcised Philistines?" But Samson answered his father, "Get her for me, for she is the one I want." ⁴Now his father and mother did not know that this had been brought about by the LORD, who was seeking an opportunity against the Philistines; for at that time they ruled over Israel.

The Philistines were part of a larger group that migrated into the eastern Mediterranean region toward the end of the thirteenth century BCE. The Philistines settled on the coast of Canaan. Unlike other groups in Judges who raided Israelite areas to take the harvest, the Philistines wanted land. Having acquired the skill of forging iron before the Israelites, they were a serious threat. The Philistines were defeated by King David and his army in the tenth century BCE and were confined to the area around Gaza (2 Sam 5:17-25; 8:1).

The introduction to the story of Samson's marriage reveals two of his character flaws: he is demanding, and there is no discipline in his desire for a woman. Samson sees a woman who is from the Philistines, a group often depicted as an enemy of Israel. The two peoples were locked in a mortal struggle for possession of the land. The Philistines had the technological advantage: they knew how to smelt iron. Samson desires a Philistine woman, and his parents cannot persuade him to pursue an Isra-

elite woman instead. Samson says to his father, "Get her for me." His attitude warns that this marriage will be difficult.

Judges 14:5-20

⁵So Samson went down to Timnah with his father and mother. When he turned aside to the vineyards of Timnah, a young lion came roaring out toward him. ⁶But the spirit of the LORD rushed upon Samson, and he tore the lion apart barehanded, as one tears a young goat. Without telling his father or mother what he had done, ⁷he went down and spoke to the woman. He liked her. ⁸Later, when he came back to marry her, he turned aside to look at the remains of the lion, and there was a swarm of bees in the lion's carcass, and honey. ⁹So he scooped the honey out into his hands and ate it as he went along. When he came to his father and mother, he gave them some to eat, but he did not tell them that he had scooped the honey from the lion's carcass.

¹⁰His father also went down to the woman, and Samson gave a feast there, since it was customary for the young men to do this. ¹¹Out of their fear of him, they brought thirty men to be his companions. ¹²Samson said to them, "Let me propose a riddle to you. If within the seven days of the feast you solve it for me, I will give you thirty linen tunics and thirty sets of garments. ¹³But if you cannot answer it for me, you must give me thirty tunics and thirty sets of garments." "Propose your riddle," they responded, "and we will listen to it." ¹⁴So he said to them,

"Out of the eater came food,
    out of the strong came sweetness."

For three days they were unable to answer the riddle, ¹⁵and on the fourth day they said to Samson's wife, "Trick your husband into solving the riddle for us, or we will burn you and your family. Did you invite us here to reduce us to poverty?" ¹⁶So Samson's wife wept at his side and said, "You just hate me! You do not love me! You proposed a riddle to my people, but did not tell me the answer." He said to her, "If I did not tell even my father or my mother, must I tell you?" [17]But she wept beside him during the seven days the feast lasted, and on the seventh day, he told her the answer, because she pressed him, and she explained the riddle to her people.

[18]On the seventh day, before the sun set, the men of the city said to him,

"What is sweeter than honey,
    what is stronger than a lion?"

He replied to them,

"If you had not plowed with my heifer,
    you would not have solved my riddle."

[19]The spirit of the LORD rushed upon him, and he went down to Ashkelon, where he killed thirty of their men and stripped them; he gave their garments to those who had answered the riddle. Then he went off to his own family in anger, [20]and Samson's wife was married to the companion who had been his best man.

Samson has his way and the wedding to the Philistine woman takes place. During the celebration he makes a wager. He thinks he cannot lose. The riddle he proposes is based not on common human experience but on his own particular experience. No one could know the answer. In this sense the wager is unfair. The young Philistine men find that indeed they cannot solve the riddle by wit, so they turn to another method, pressuring the bride. They threaten her life and the lives of her family. The woman is put in an impossible situation. She has to choose between the demands of her own people and loyalty to her new husband. She has to consider whether she and her family will be protected by Samson or by the Philistines. Where should her loyalty be? Where is safety for her?

Whether out of fear or loyalty, she chooses to trust her own people, the Philistines. She coaxes the solution from Samson and reveals the secret to her countrymen. They answer Samson riddle for riddle. Their riddle demonstrates knowledge of his experience with the honeycomb in the carcass of the lion. (Note that in touching the lion's carcass, Samson has already broken his nazirite vow.) Samson knows that his bride has to be the source of the information. His response again reveals his character. He kills thirty men and pays off his wager with their clothes. Then he returns home in anger.

What of the bride? Her wedding has turned into a disaster. She was promised in marriage to a violent, demanding man from an enemy people. He used the wedding celebration to instigate a fight between his people and hers. She is forced to choose sides. Her choice wins the wager for some of her countrymen, but causes the death of others. With the angry departure of her bridegroom, she is given in marriage to another man, probably still without consideration for her feelings. She is a tragic figure, the victim of a ruthless culture.

Judges 15:1-8

[1]After some time, in the season of the wheat harvest, Samson visited his wife, bringing a young goat. But when he said, "Let me go into my wife's room," her father would not let him go in. [2]He said, "I thought you hated her, so I gave her to your best man. Her younger sister is better; you may have her instead." [3]Samson said to him, "This time I am guiltless if I harm the Philistines." [4]So Samson went and caught three hundred jackals, and turning them tail to tail, he took some torches and tied one between each pair of tails. [5]He then kindled the torches and set the jackals loose in the standing grain of the Philistines, thus burning both the shocks and standing grain, the vineyards and olive groves.

[6]When the Philistines asked, "Who has done this?" they were told, "Samson, the son-in-law of the Timnite, because his wife was taken and given to his best man." So the Philistines went up and destroyed her and her family by fire. [7]Samson said to them, "If this is how you act, I will not stop until I have taken revenge on you." [8]And he struck them hip and thigh—a great slaughter. Then he went down and stayed in a cleft of the crag of Etam.

Samson has not forgotten his bride. After some time he returns to Timnah to consummate his marriage. The woman's father informs him that it is too late; she is married to another man. Instead, he offers Samson another woman, his younger daughter. Samson again becomes enraged. He burns the whole wheat harvest along with the vineyards and olive orchards. In retaliation the Philistines carry out the threat made earlier (14:15). They burn his would-be bride along with her whole family. Samson's response is to slaughter yet more Philistines.

Thus this woman and her family suffer a horrible death. Her only active part in the tragedy was to make a choice for the Philistines, her own people, and against Samson, her husband. The choice was made under compulsion; either choice would have destroyed her. She is destroyed in the enmity between two peoples. Her death symbolizes the subjugation of the Philistines by the Israelites.

The Bible is marked with scenes of violence (as in the story of Samson). The violence exacted against women is often particularly cruel. The United States Conference of Catholic Bishops condemns all **violence against women**, especially domestic violence, in their document *When I Call for Help:* "[V]iolence against women, inside or outside the home, is *never* justified. Violence in any form—physical, sexual, psychological, or verbal—is sinful" (Introduction).

DELILAH

Judges 16:1-22

[1]Once Samson went to Gaza, where he saw a prostitute and visited her. [2]The people of Gaza were told, "Samson has come here," and they surrounded him with an ambush at the city gate all night long. And all the night they waited, saying, "At morning light we will kill him." [3]Samson lay there until midnight. Then he rose at midnight, seized the doors of the city gate and the two gateposts, and tore them loose, bar and all. He hoisted them on his shoulders and carried them to the top of the ridge opposite Hebron.

[4]After that he fell in love with a woman in the Wadi Sorek whose name was Delilah. [5]The lords of the Philistines came up to her and said, "Trick him and find out where he gets his great strength, and how we may overcome and bind him so as to make him helpless. Then for our part, we will each give you eleven hundred pieces of silver."

[6]So Delilah said to Samson, "Tell me where you get your great strength and how you may be bound so as to be made helpless." [7]"If they bind me with seven fresh bowstrings that have not dried," Samson answered her, "I shall grow weaker and be like anyone else." [8]So the lords of the Philistines brought her seven fresh bowstrings that had not dried, and she bound him with them. [9]She had men lying in wait in the room, and she said to him, "The Philistines are upon you, Samson!" But he snapped the bowstrings as a thread of tow is snapped by a whiff of flame; and his strength remained unexplained.

[10]Delilah said to Samson, "You have mocked me and told me lies. Now tell me how you may be bound." [11]"If they bind me tight with new ropes, with which no work has been done," he answered her, "I shall grow weaker and be like anyone else." [12]So Delilah took new ropes and bound him with them. Then she said to him, "The Philistines are upon you, Samson!" For there were men lying in wait in the room. But he snapped the ropes off his arms like thread.

[13]Delilah said to Samson again, "Up to now you have mocked me and told me lies. Tell me how you may be bound." He said to her, "If you weave the seven locks of my hair into the web and fasten them with the pin, I shall grow weaker and be like anyone else." [14]So when he went to bed, Delilah took the seven locks of his hair and wove them into the web, and fastened them with the pin. Then she said, "The Philistines are upon you,

Samson!" Awakening from his sleep, he pulled out both the loom and the web.

¹⁵Then she said to him, "How can you say 'I love you' when your heart is not mine? Three times already you have mocked me, and not told me where you get your great strength!" ¹⁶She pressed him continually and pestered him till he was deathly weary of it. ¹⁷So he told her all that was in his heart and said, "No razor has touched my head, for I have been a nazirite for God from my mother's womb. If I am shaved, my strength will leave me, and I shall grow weaker and be like anyone else." ¹⁸When Delilah realized that he had told her all that was in his heart, she summoned the lords of the Philistines, saying, "Come up this time, for he has told me all that is in his heart." So the lords of the Philistines came to her and brought the money with them. ¹⁹She put him to sleep on her lap, and called for a man who shaved off the seven locks of his hair. He immediately became helpless, for his strength had left him. ²⁰When she said "The Philistines are upon you, Samson!" he woke from his sleep and thought, "I will go out as I have done time and again and shake myself free." He did not realize that the LORD had left him. ²¹But the Philistines seized him and gouged out his eyes. Then they brought him down to Gaza and bound him with bronze fetters, and he was put to grinding grain in the prison. ²²But the hair of his head began to grow as soon as it was shaved.

Judges 16 begins with a story of Samson and a prostitute. The narrative continues to remind us of Samson's weakness for women. The brief story of the prostitute introduces the story of Delilah, a woman who proves to be stronger than Samson.

In this story of many women, she is the only one named and the only one whom Samson is said to love. She is placed in a situation similar to that of Samson's bride in Judges 14. The Philistines want to use her to gain the secret of Samson's strength. They do not threaten her as they did the bride, however. Instead, they promise her a great deal of money.

Three times Delilah attempts to learn Samson's secret. Each time the Philistines act on the information she gives them. Each time Samson has deceived her. Thus when she begs him the fourth time to reveal the secret to her, he must know that she will again betray him to the Philistines. But Samson cannot resist her pleading, just as he could not resist the pleading of his bride. Both women pose the question as a test of love: "How can you say 'I love you' when your heart is not mine?" (16:15; cf. 14:16). Finally Samson opens his heart to Delilah. His strength comes from his consecration to God; his long hair is the sign of that consecration. A fourth time Delilah summons the Philistines who cut his hair, blind him, and imprison him. It seems that this is the end of Samson's strength. But his hair grows back, and his strength returns. As the story continues, the Philistines gather in the temple of their god Dagon to celebrate the capture of Samson. They chain Samson between two of the supporting columns. After a prayer to God for strength, he pulls down the columns and with them the temple. Samson destroys more Philistines with his death than in his lifetime (16:23-30).

Delilah is often seen as a heartless woman who uses the power of love and sexuality to destroy a man, a woman to whom money is worth more than love. It is possible, however, that she knows the fate of the other Philistine women involved with Samson. Perhaps she betrays Samson in order to save her own life. Perhaps her motive is loyalty to the Philistines. If this story were told by the Philistines, she would be seen as a hero. The story does not report Delilah's reasons, making her one of the most cryptic and complex characters in the story of Samson.

CONTINUING THE CONVERSATION

By Jaime L. Waters

Jael: The Complexity of Women in War

Is Jael a warrior or a villain? Should we condemn her for murder or praise her for decisive action? Interpreters are divided in how to handle Jael, which shows the complexity of the biblical traditions about her. Nowell states that the story of Jael offends many readers because of its violence, perhaps especially because that violence is executed by a woman. My reading of Jael is different, as I would suggest that we view Jael in a positive light. My assessment is not to suggest that readers should emulate Jael's violent actions. Yet, in her biblical context, Jael exhibits power and bravery. Her actions advance the covenantal promise of land for the Israelites, which is likely why Judges remembers her as a blessed woman (5:24).

The Context of War

In the book of Judges, one of the most violent books in the Old Testament, the Israelites are described as engaging in wars to try to claim the land that has been promised to them by God. For readers who are uneasy with the traditions of Judges, it is important to keep in mind that the historical realities and the literary depictions in Scripture may not be aligned. Judges, like Joshua, is telling a complex and violent community history, and in this context, violence is viewed as necessary and even divinely mandated in order for Israel to attain the promised land.

Judges 4 provides a setup for war, as the Israelites again have been unfaithful to their covenantal obligations. The prophet Deborah is called to be a judge and lead a military campaign against the Canaanites. Sisera is one of the commanders of the Canaanite army, and Deborah proclaims that "it is into a woman's power that the LORD is going to sell Sisera" (4:9).

As Sisera flees battle, he happens upon Jael. Jael's ethnic origin is not stated, but she is the wife of Heber the Kenite, so presumably she is also a Kenite. The Kenites have ties to the Israelites through Moses' father-in-law (4:11), but the Kenites also had positive relationships with Jabin, the Canaanite king (4:17). Sisera may have viewed Jael as either an ally or at least not a threat, so he enters her tent when she tells him not to fear. She is hospitable to him and gives him milk, and he instructs her to lie if someone comes looking for him. While he sleeps, Jael uses a hammer and drives a tent peg into his head, killing him. She then reports to the Israelite commander Barak that she will bring him to find the person he seeks. After the event, the text affirms that God subdued Jabin, the king of the Canaanites, and the Israelites destroyed him (4:23).

Jael's Motives

Jael takes advantage of the opportunity to kill a leader who is against the Israelites. She is strategic in getting him to come into her tent, and she makes him comfortable before her act. Jael shows decisiveness, but we should not miss the fact that we hear very little from her in the narrative, and we have to fill in some gaps to assess her motivations.

Beyond being a decisive warrior, Jael might also be protecting herself, a possibility that becomes evident in Judges 5 and at the end of the book of Judges. Within the context of war, women were especially vulnerable to rape, abduction, and death. The end of Judges depicts women being raped, dismembered, and abducted as wives (see Judg 19–21). As a woman living in close proximity to warring communities, Jael could have been vulnerable to these kinds of assaults. Her attack on Sisera might be interpreted as preempting his attack on her.

Judges 5, the song of Deborah, alludes to this possibility. The text is one of the oldest in the Old Testament, dating near the time of the events it records. The song fills in details and offers alternative images of what might have happened. The end of the song includes images of war, noting that men at war divide what is captured, with a "woman or two for every man" (5:30).[10] With these images of sexual violence in mind, we might be called to see Jael's vulnerability as a woman alone in the context of war, which helps to situate and interpret her actions in a different light.

As we think about these different portraits, we can see the biblical tradition's diversity in reflecting on Jael. The later prose narrative of Judges 4 depicts Jael in a more decisive way, like an assassin setting Sisera up before killing him. In the older poetic account of Judges 5, Jael's vulnerability might be highlighted by invoking images of women as spoils of war. Both Judges 4 and 5 celebrate Jael's actions as a fulfillment of Deborah's prophecy and a pivotal action that helped Israel defeat the Canaanites.

EXPLORING LESSON FOUR

1. In what ways does Rahab prove that her faith outweighs her reputation as a "harlot" (Josh 2:1-21)?

_____

_____

_____

_____

_____

2. Why do you suppose the biblical writers recorded Rahab's occupation (Josh 2:1; 6:25) and listed her as one of the few women in the genealogy of Jesus (Matt 1:5)?

_____

_____

_____

_____

_____

3. By what authority does Deborah plan and direct Israel's military leaders into battle (Judg 4:4-9)? According to the commentary, how is she different from other judges of Israel?

_____

_____

_____

_____

_____

4. According to the poetic version of the battle between the Canaanites and the Israelites, what forces contributed to Israel's victory (Judg 5:3-5, 13-18, 21-22)?

_____

_____

_____

_____

_____

5. What is your gut reaction to Jael's treatment of Sisera (Judg 4:17-22; 5:24-27)? And to Deborah singing of Sisera's mother watching for him to return from battle (Judg 5:28-30)? What was the overall message of these stories for the people of Israel?

_____

_____

_____

_____

_____

6. Jephthah bargained with the Lord for military power and then seemed powerless to save his daughter from a fate that he created (Judg 11:29-40). When have you wanted something so badly, only to discover it was not worth the price to yourself or others?

_____

_____

_____

_____

7. Samson is often collectively remembered as a pitiable, tragic figure. But how does the book of Judges depict Samson? What words would you use to describe his character and actions?

_____

_____

_____

_____

_____

8. Samson's abuse of women and use of them to barter for power over his enemies is matched by Delilah's craftiness on behalf of her people, the Philistines (Judg 14–16). At the time, each would have been seen by their own people as heroes. What does this tell us about how our assessment of others can be colored by our own origins, cultures, and interests?

_____

_____

_____

_____

_____

9. Seemingly impossible situations often put us in positions that feel unbearable. We might feel we must choose between the lesser of two evils (as was the case with some of the women in this lesson). How might we seek God's guidance in such times? And how might we assist others in their "impossible" situations with the best of our gifts and abilities?

_____

_____

_____

_____

_____

_____

10. Continuing the Conversation: Does this essay shed any new light on Jael and her situation for you? Does a fuller awareness of the violence of the times and the nature of biblical writings in Judges help you understand Jael's story? If so, in what way?

_____

_____

_____

_____

_____

_____

CLOSING PRAYER

Prayer

Jephthah made a vow to the LORD. "If you deliver the Ammonites into my power . . ."

(Judg 11:30)

O God, you are the source of all power. We deceive ourselves when we believe anything is accomplished on our own. Teach us your ways so our words may be true and our actions may conform to your will. We pray for forgiveness for the abuse of power, around the world and in our own lives. Heal what is violent in our world, especially . . .

LESSON FIVE

More Women of Israel's Early Tribes

Begin your personal study and group discussion with a simple and sincere prayer such as:

Prayer

God of Salvation, in these stories of biblical women, may we discover in ourselves a fresh desire to know and love you. Continue to form us as a people of your own.

Read pages 92–103, Lesson Five.

Respond to the questions on pages 104–106, Exploring Lesson Five.

The Closing Prayer on page 107 is for your personal use and may be used at the end of group discussion.

The Book of Ruth

CHAPTER 1

Naomi Loses Her Husband and Sons

¹Once back in the time of the judges there was a famine in the land; so a man from Bethlehem of Judah left home with his wife and two sons to reside on the plateau of Moab. ²The man was named Elimelech, his wife Naomi, and his sons Mahlon and Chilion; they were Ephrathites from Bethlehem of Judah. Some time after their arrival on the plateau of Moab, ³Elimelech, the husband of Naomi, died, and she was left with her two sons. ⁴They married Moabite women, one named Orpah, the other Ruth. When they had lived there about ten years, ⁵both Mahlon and Chilion died also, and the woman was left with neither her two boys nor her husband.

Naomi and Ruth Return to Bethlehem

⁶She and her daughters-in-law then prepared to go back from the plateau of Moab because word had reached her there that the LORD had seen to his people's needs and given them food. ⁷She and her two daughters-in-law left the place where they had been living. On the road back to the land of Judah, ⁸Naomi said to her daughters-in-law, "Go back, each of you to your mother's house. May the LORD show you the same kindness as you have shown to the deceased and to me. ⁹May the LORD guide each of you to find a husband and a home in which you will be at rest." She kissed them good-bye, but they wept aloud, ¹⁰crying, "No! We will go back with you, to your people." ¹¹Naomi replied, "Go back, my daughters. Why come with me? Have I other sons in my womb who could become your husbands? ¹²Go, my daughters, for I am too old to marry again. Even if I had any such hope, or if tonight I had a husband and were to bear sons, ¹³would you wait for them and deprive yourselves of husbands until those sons grew up? No, my daughters, my lot is too bitter for you, because the LORD has extended his hand against me." ¹⁴Again they wept aloud; then Orpah kissed her mother-in-law good-bye, but Ruth clung to her.

Scripture excerpts are found in shaded text boxes throughout the lesson.

MORE WOMEN OF ISRAEL'S EARLY TRIBES

As Israel's tribal period continues, we encounter women whose lives are deeply intertwined with one another. Themes of loyalty and rivalry, fertility and infertility, and abiding faith in God continue to punctuate these biblical texts.

Three Widows in the Book of Ruth

Three women are introduced in the first chapter of the book of Ruth: Naomi, Ruth, and Orpah. They are the survivors of the family of Elimelech. All the men have died. The three women face the same problem: the need to sustain themselves and thrive with limited financial resources. Their options were remarriage, begging, or prostitution. Israelite society expected a widow to marry within the family of her dead husband, as in the story of Tamar in Genesis 38 (see Lesson Two), or to return to her father's house. The law commanded Israelites to be charitable to widows, along with strangers and orphans (Deut 14:28-29; 24:17-21).

ORPAH

Ruth 1:1-22

Orpah is a Moabite woman, the widow of Chilion, the daughter-in-law of Elimelech and Naomi. She has risked marriage with a foreigner. Along with the misery of her own childlessness, she has suffered the death of her husband, her father-in-law, and her brother-in-law. As the story opens, she is beginning a journey with her mother-in-law to a strange place where her people are not welcome (cf. Deut 23:4-7).

The mother-in-law, Naomi, insists that the two daughters-in-law should return home. She cannot support them; she has no other sons who can marry them. She can promise them nothing in her own land. She sends them back to their *mother's* house (1:8), a noteworthy designation in a society where a house normally belonged to the father. Orpah heeds her mother-in-law's words and in sorrow kisses her goodbye. She returns to the land of Moab.

In Hebrew the term for **widow** is literally associated with silence or the inability to speak. A widow was particularly vulnerable; without a husband, she had no voice and had to rely on her father or her son. Without these male relatives, without an inheritance, and usually unable to operate in the public sphere, each widow became a potential drain on the larger community.

Widows and orphans became symbolic of those on the fringes of society, exploited and even oppressed. The fact that Israel's law had to articulate protection of widows (Exod 22:21-22; Deut 24:17) is likely evidence that such protection was necessary.

Because the story follows the life of Ruth, Orpah has often been neglected or even scorned by commentators. Her own virtues, however, deserve to be considered. She acts out of genuine love for her mother-in-law. She remains with Naomi after her husband's death; she begins

[15]"See now," she said, "your sister-in-law has gone back to her people and her god. Go back after your sister-in-law!" [16]But Ruth said, "Do not press me to go back and abandon you!

Wherever you go I will go,
    wherever you lodge I will lodge.
Your people shall be my people
    and your God, my God.
[17]Where you die I will die,
    and there be buried.

May the Lord do thus to me, and more, if even death separates me from you!" [18]Naomi then ceased to urge her, for she saw she was determined to go with her.

[19]So they went on together until they reached Bethlehem. On their arrival there, the whole town was excited about them, and the women asked: "Can this be Naomi?" [20]But she said to them, "Do not call me Naomi ['Sweet']. Call me Mara ['Bitter'], for the Almighty has made my life very bitter. [21]I went away full, but the Lord has brought me back empty. Why should you call me 'Sweet,' since the Lord has brought me to trial, and the Almighty has pronounced evil sentence on me." [22]Thus it was that Naomi came back with her Moabite daughter-in-law Ruth, who accompanied her back from the plateau of Moab. They arrived in Bethlehem at the beginning of the barley harvest.

continue

the journey back to her husband's native land. There is no future for her in either of these actions. What motive can there be except love for the family into which she has married?

Orpah heeds the wisdom of her mother-in-law and obeys her. She will not be a burden to Naomi. She returns to her mother's house. The departure with tears and kisses certainly demonstrates the love between Orpah and Naomi.

Orpah is a good daughter-in-law—loving, caring, and obedient toward her mother-in-law Naomi.

CHAPTER 2

Ruth Meets Boaz in the Grain Field

[1]Naomi had a powerful relative named Boaz, through the clan of her husband Elimelech. [2]Ruth the Moabite said to Naomi, "I would like to go and glean grain in the field of anyone who will allow me." Naomi said to her, "Go ahead, my daughter." [3]So she went. The field she entered to glean after the harvesters happened to be the section belonging to Boaz, of the clan of Elimelech. [4]Soon, along came Boaz from Bethlehem and said to the harvesters, "The LORD be with you," and they replied, "The LORD bless you." [5]Boaz asked the young man overseeing his harvesters, "Whose young woman is this?" [6]The young man overseeing the harvesters answered, "She is the young Moabite who came back with Naomi from the plateau of Moab. [7]She said, 'I would like to gather the gleanings into sheaves after the harvesters.' Ever since she came this morning she has remained here until now, with scarcely a moment's rest."

[8]Boaz then spoke to Ruth, "Listen, my daughter. Do not go to glean in anyone else's field; you are not to leave here. Stay here with my young women. [9]Watch to see which field is to be harvested, and follow them. Have I not commanded the young men to do you no harm? When you are thirsty, go and drink from the vessels the young people have filled." [10]Casting herself prostrate upon the ground, she said to him, "Why should I, a foreigner, be favored with your attention?" [11]Boaz answered her: "I have had a complete account of what you have done for your mother-in-law after your husband's death; you have left your father and your mother and the land of your birth, and have come to a people whom previously you did not know. [12]May the LORD reward what you have done! May you receive a full reward from the LORD, the God of Israel, under whose wings you have come for refuge." [13]She said, "May I prove worthy of your favor, my lord. You have comforted me. You have spoken to the heart of your servant—and I am not even one of your servants!" [14]At mealtime Boaz said to her, "Come

NAOMI

Ruth 2:1-23

Naomi is the primary actor in the story of Ruth. When she is introduced she seems to be a powerless person, a widow who has lost not only her husband but both of her sons (1:1-5). In addition, Naomi is a sojourner in a strange land. All she has is the love and faithfulness of two daughters-in-law. Yet she is a competent, inventive woman who makes the best of whatever life offers her.

Naomi returns to her hometown of Bethlehem, accompanied by one daughter-in-law. The bitterness of her experience is revealed in her comment to the women of Bethlehem: "Do not call me Naomi ['Sweet']. Call me Mara ['Bitter'], for the Almighty has made my life very bitter" (1:20). She lays the responsibility for her distress squarely at the feet of God. "The Almighty has pronounced evil sentence on me" (1:21).

Naomi's tragic situation does not cause her to give up, however. Throughout the story she is definitely the one in charge. Ruth asks her permission to glean, and Naomi expects a full report when she returns (2:2, 19). Naomi immediately sees the opportunity with Boaz and plans the event at the threshing floor (3:1-6). Again, Ruth does just as her mother-in-law instructs and returns to report the results (3:16-17).

 Gleaning—or the gathering of leftover grain after a harvest—was a form of distributive justice (the distribution of social and economic resources for the common good of all) in biblical times. The social nature of the human person, the common good, and access to what meets basic human needs continues to present a fundamental challenge in our world.

Naomi knows how to wait. After Ruth returns from the threshing floor, Naomi instructs, "Wait here, my daughter, until you learn what happens, for the man will not rest, but will

settle the matter today" (3:18). At the end of the story, it is Naomi who is the beneficiary. The neighbor women say to Naomi, "Blessed is the LORD who has not failed to provide you today with a redeemer [NAB: heir]" (4:14). She claims the child born to Ruth and Boaz, placing him on her lap and becoming his nurse. The neighbor women name him Obed when they hear a grandson is born to Naomi (4:17).

Naomi weaves together the lives of all the characters in the story. She is wife, mother, mother-in-law. She is friend, so loved that one daughter-in-law refuses to leave her and the other sobs as she departs. She is relative to Boaz and knows his character. She is neighbor to the women of Bethlehem, and they continue to be interested in her affairs. She is grandmother to baby Obed and great-great-grandmother of King David. The story happens all around her, and she is influential in shaping its events.

RUTH

Ruth 3:1-18

Ruth is the widowed daughter-in-law of a widowed mother-in-law, a woman surrounded by death. She is a foreigner in Israel. Worse, she is a Moabite. Deuteronomy prescribes, "No Ammonite or Moabite may ever come into the assembly of the LORD, nor may any of their descendants even to the tenth generation come into the assembly of the LORD, because they would not come to meet you with food and water on your journey after you left Egypt, and because they hired Balaam, son of Beor, from Pethor in Aram Naharaim, to curse you. The LORD, your God, would not listen to Balaam but turned his curse into a blessing for you, because the LORD, your God, loves you. Never seek their welfare or prosperity as long as you live" (Deut 23:4-7; cf. Neh 13:1-3, 23-25).

Ruth is undaunted by this situation, however. She faithfully follows her beloved mother-in-law. She speaks the words that have become a well-known testimony to undying love:

here and have something to eat; dip your bread in the sauce." Then as she sat near the harvesters, he handed her some roasted grain and she ate her fill and had some left over. [15]As she rose to glean, Boaz instructed his young people: "Let her glean among the sheaves themselves without scolding her, [16]and even drop some handfuls and leave them for her to glean; do not rebuke her."

[17]She gleaned in the field until evening, and when she beat out what she had gleaned it came to about an ephah of barley, [18]which she took into the town and showed to her mother-in-law. Next she brought out what she had left over from the meal and gave it to her. [19]So her mother-in-law said to her, "Where did you glean today? Where did you go to work? May the one who took notice of you be blessed!" Then she told her mother-in-law with whom she had worked. "The man at whose place I worked today is named Boaz," she said. [20]"May he be blessed by the LORD, who never fails to show kindness to the living and to the dead," Naomi exclaimed to her daughter-in-law. She continued, "This man is a near relative of ours, one of our redeemers." [21]"He even told me," added Ruth the Moabite, "Stay with my young people until they complete my entire harvest." [22]"You would do well, my daughter," Naomi rejoined, "to work with his young women; in someone else's field you might be insulted." [23]So she stayed gleaning with Boaz's young women until the end of the barley and wheat harvests.

CHAPTER 3

Ruth and Boaz at the Threshing Floor

When Ruth was back with her mother-in-law, [1]Naomi said to her, "My daughter, should I not be seeking a pleasing home for you? [2]Now! Is not Boaz, whose young women you were working with, a relative of ours? This very night he will be winnowing barley at the threshing floor. [3]Now, go bathe and anoint yourself; then put on your best attire and go down to the threshing floor. Do not make yourself known to the man before he

continue

has finished eating and drinking. ⁴But when he lies down, take note of the place where he lies; then go uncover a place at his feet and you lie down. He will then tell you what to do." ⁵"I will do whatever you say," Ruth replied. ⁶She went down to the threshing floor and did just as her mother-in-law had instructed her.

⁷Boaz ate and drank to his heart's content, and went to lie down at the edge of the pile of grain. She crept up, uncovered a place at his feet, and lay down. ⁸Midway through the night, the man gave a start and groped about, only to find a woman lying at his feet. ⁹"Who are you?" he asked. She replied, "I am your servant Ruth. Spread the wing of your cloak over your servant, for you are a redeemer." ¹⁰He said, "May the Lord bless you, my daughter! You have been even more loyal now than before in not going after the young men, whether poor or rich. ¹¹Now rest assured, my daughter, I will do for you whatever you say; all my townspeople know you to be a worthy woman.

¹²Now, I am in fact a redeemer, but there is another redeemer closer than I. ¹³Stay where you are for tonight, and tomorrow, if he will act as redeemer for you, good. But if he will not, as the Lord lives, I will do it myself. Lie there until morning." ¹⁴So she lay at his feet until morning, but rose before anyone could recognize another, for Boaz had said, "Let it not be known that this woman came to the threshing floor." ¹⁵Then he said to her, "Take off the shawl you are wearing; hold it firmly." When she did so, he poured out six measures of barley and helped her lift the bundle; then he himself left for the town.

¹⁶She, meanwhile, went home to her mother-in-law, who asked, "How did things go, my daughter?" So she told her all the man had done for her, ¹⁷and concluded, "He gave me these six measures of barley and said, 'Do not go back to your mother-in-law empty.'" ¹⁸Naomi then said, "Wait here, my daughter, until you learn what happens, for the man will not rest, but will settle the matter today."

Ruth and Boaz

Wherever you go I will go,
    Wherever you lodge I will lodge.
Your people shall be my people
    And your God, my God.
Where you die I will die,
    And there be buried. (1:16-17)

Ruth goes to work to support herself and Naomi (2:2). She is diligent, working "with scarcely a moment's rest" (2:7). She is humble. When Boaz, the owner of the field, speaks kindly to her, she replies: "Why should I, a foreigner, be favored with your attention?" (2:10). She is generous. She brings her mother-in-law not only what she has gleaned, but even what she had saved from lunch (2:17-18).

Ruth is brave and daring. When Naomi conceives the plan to remind Boaz that he could fulfill the levirate obligation (Lev 25:25) by marrying Ruth, she obeys without question. She does exactly what her mother-in-law suggests. She bathes and anoints herself, puts on her best clothes, and goes to the threshing floor at night. There she uncovers the sleeping Boaz and lies down at his feet. Her actions are unexpected, and she puts herself at considerable risk. How safe is a woman, a foreigner besides, alone at night at a threshing floor where the men have been drinking?

Boaz, however, has become Ruth's protector (see 2:8-9, 15). When she informs him that he is her next of kin, he blesses her. He credits her with *hesed*, the covenant virtue of loyal love, for heeding her mother-in-law rather than "going after the young men." He adds that the townspeople know that she is "a worthy woman." Even though Ruth is a Moabite, Boaz recognizes that she demonstrates Israelite covenantal loyalty.

Boaz needs to settle a prior claim; there is a still closer relative than he. So he sends Ruth away from the threshing floor before anyone can recognize her and spread gossip. But he does not send her home empty-handed. She returns to Naomi not only with the news, but with a cloak full of barley. Then with Naomi she waits while the men settle the legal matters.

Happy Ending

Ruth 4:1-22

Boaz settles the prior claim and marries Ruth. The witnesses bless her in the names of three great women: Rachel and Leah, who "between them built up the house of Israel" and Tamar, who "bore [Perez] to Judah" (4:11-12). The blessing of the witnesses is fulfilled. As Rachel and Leah were the mothers of Israel's twelve tribes, Ruth becomes the great-grandmother of David, Israel's greatest king. Like Tamar, Ruth is a foreign woman who acted unconventionally in order to fulfill the levirate obligation to her dead husband. Like Perez, Ruth's son Obed continues the line of the covenant people.

The neighbor women also praise Ruth. They rejoice with Naomi in the daughter-in-law who loves her: "She is worth more to you than seven sons!" Seven is the number of fullness or

CHAPTER 4

Boaz Marries Ruth

¹Boaz went to the gate and took a seat there. Along came the other redeemer of whom he had spoken. Boaz called to him by name, "Come, sit here." And he did so. ²Then Boaz picked out ten of the elders of the town and asked them to sit nearby. When they had done this, ³he said to the other redeemer: "Naomi, who has come back from the plateau of Moab, is putting up for sale the piece of land that belonged to our kinsman Elimelech. ⁴So I thought I would inform you. Before those here present, including the elders of my people, purchase the field; act as redeemer. But if you do not want to do it, tell me so, that I may know, for no one has a right of redemption prior to yours, and mine is next." He answered, "I will act as redeemer."

⁵Boaz continued, "When you acquire the field from Naomi, you also acquire responsibility for Ruth the Moabite, the widow of the late heir, to raise up a family for the deceased on his estate." ⁶The redeemer replied, "I cannot exercise my right of redemption for that would endanger my own estate. You do it in my place, for I cannot." ⁷Now it used to be the custom in Israel that, to make binding a contract of redemption or exchange, one party would take off a sandal and give it to the other. This was the form of attestation in Israel. ⁸So the other redeemer, in saying to Boaz, "Acquire it for yourself," drew off his sandal. ⁹Boaz then said to the elders and to all the people, "You are witnesses today that I have acquired from Naomi all the holdings of Elimelech, Chilion and Mahlon. ¹⁰I also acquire Ruth the Moabite, the widow of Mahlon, as my wife, in order to raise up a family for her late husband on his estate, so that the name of the deceased may not perish from his people and his place. Do you witness this today?" ¹¹All those at the gate, including the elders, said, "We do. May the LORD make this woman come into your house like Rachel and Leah, who

continue

between them built up the house of Israel. Prosper in Ephrathah! Bestow a name in Bethlehem! ¹²With the offspring the LORD will give you from this young woman, may your house become like the house of Perez, whom Tamar bore to Judah."

Naomi Gains a Son

¹³Boaz took Ruth. When they came together as husband and wife, the LORD enabled her to conceive and she bore a son. ¹⁴Then the women said to Naomi, "Blessed is the LORD who has not failed to provide you today with a redeemer. May he become famous in Israel! ¹⁵He will restore your life and be the support of your old age, for his mother is the daughter-in-law who loves you. She is worth more to you than seven sons!" ¹⁶Naomi took the boy, cradled him against her breast, and cared for him. ¹⁷The neighbor women joined the celebration: "A son has been born to Naomi!" They named him Obed. He was the father of Jesse, the father of David.

The Genealogy of David

¹⁸These are the descendants of Perez: Perez was the father of Hezron, ¹⁹Hezron was the father of Ram, Ram was the father of Amminadab, ²⁰Amminadab was the father of Nahshon, Nahshon was the father of Salma, ²¹Salma was the father of Boaz, Boaz was the father of Obed, ²²Obed was the father of Jesse, and Jesse became the father of David.

completion. There can be no greater praise than this in a society where a woman's worth and survival were dependent on sons.

Ruth is a foreign woman, a Moabite, who not only practices covenant virtues but becomes a mother of the covenant people. The devoted love between Ruth and Naomi, two childless and seemingly powerless widows, gives rise to the line of David whose dynasty, God promises, will endure forever (2 Sam 7:16). In Matthew's genealogy, which identifies Jesus as Son of David, Ruth is listed as one of his female ancestors (Matt 1:5).

Ruth and Naomi

The genealogy at the end of the book of Ruth identifies Ruth and Boaz as ancestors of David, and thus of Jesus (see Matt 1:5-6). Because **Bethlehem** is the hometown of Naomi and the adopted town of Ruth, it comes to be known as David's city and is ultimately associated with the birth of Jesus (Matt 2:5-6; John 7:42).

HANNAH AND PENINNAH

1 Samuel 1:1-8

¹There was a certain man from Ramathaim, a Zuphite from the hill country of Ephraim. His name was Elkanah, the son of Jeroham, son of Elihu, son of Tohu, son of Zuph, an Ephraimite. ²He had two wives, one named Hannah, the other Peninnah; Peninnah had children, but Hannah had no children. ³Each year this man went up from his city to worship and offer sacrifice to the LORD of hosts at Shiloh, where the two sons of Eli, Hophni and Phinehas, were ministering as priests of the LORD. ⁴When the day came for Elkanah to offer sacrifice, he used to give portions to his wife Peninnah and to all her sons and daughters, ⁵but he would give a double portion to Hannah because he loved her,

though the LORD had closed her womb. [6]Her rival, to upset her, would torment her constantly, since the LORD had closed her womb. [7]Year after year, when she went up to the house of the LORD, Peninnah would provoke her, and Hannah would weep and refuse to eat. [8]Elkanah, her husband, would say to her: "Hannah, why are you weeping? Why are you not eating? Why are you so miserable? Am I not better for you than ten sons?"

At the beginning of 1 Samuel we have another story in which the lives of women are intertwined. Elkanah of Ramathaim has two wives, one fruitful and one barren. It comes as no surprise that the one he loves more is Hannah, the barren wife. (Compare with Jacob and his two wives.) The situation pits the two women against each other. Peninnah, the fruitful wife, taunts Hannah because God has made her barren. Elkanah, to console Hannah, pleads, "Am I not better for you than ten sons?"

Peninnah appears only in the opening scene of the story (1:1-8). She is usually ignored, being seen as only a foil to Hannah. She has the blessing of many children and the sorrow of being loved less. The attention of her husband is turned to his other wife. The attention of the biblical author is also focused on Hannah. We are left to wonder what happened to Peninnah after Hannah began to have children. Did she lose even the small claim she had on her husband?

Hannah suffers also. Her husband is *not* worth more to her than ten sons. She is barren, which is challenging for anyone who desires children, and was especially difficult in a society where women's worth was measured by the number of sons they had.

1 Samuel 1:9-19

[9]Hannah rose after one such meal at Shiloh, and presented herself before the LORD; at the time Eli the priest was sitting on a chair near the doorpost of the LORD's temple. [10]In her bitterness she prayed to the LORD, weeping freely, [11]and made this vow: "O LORD of hosts, if you look with pity on the hardship of your servant, if you remember me and do not forget me, if you give your handmaid a male child, I will give him to the LORD all the days of his life. No razor shall ever touch his head." [12]As she continued praying before the LORD, Eli watched her mouth, [13]for Hannah was praying silently; though her lips were moving, her voice could not be heard. Eli, thinking she was drunk, [14]said to her, "How long will you make a drunken spectacle of yourself? Sober up from your wine!" [15]"No, my lord!" Hannah answered. "I am an unhappy woman. I have had neither wine nor liquor; I was only pouring out my heart to the LORD. [16]Do not think your servant a worthless woman; my prayer has been prompted by my deep sorrow and misery." [17]Eli said, "Go in peace, and may the God of Israel grant you what you have requested." [18]She replied, "Let your servant find favor in your eyes," and left. She went to her quarters, ate and drank with her husband, and no longer appeared downhearted. [19]Early the next morning they worshiped before the LORD, and then returned to their home in Ramah.

Elkanah and his family regularly went to worship God at the shrine where the ark of the covenant was then housed. The ark of the covenant, probably constructed during the desert period, was Israel's sign of the abiding presence of God with the people. The ark, a wooden chest, was said to contain the tablets of the law, a jar of manna, and Aaron's staff. Cherubim stood on each side as guardians; their outstretched wings over the ark formed the throne of God. During the time of the judges (ca. 1250–1000 BCE) the ark traveled from shrine to shrine. At the time of this story, the ark was at Shiloh.

On one of the family's regular pilgrimages Hannah went into the shrine to pray before the ark. She poured out her grief to God and asked for a son. She promised that if God answered her prayer she would dedicate this son to God as a perpetual nazirite, similar to Samson and his mother in Judges 13 (see Lesson Four). Eli, the priest who served the ark, could not understand what Hannah was doing at the shrine. She clearly was not offering a sacrifice, the common mode of worship. She was making no sound. Only her lips were moving. Eli concluded that she was drunk and scolded her for acting inappropriately in the presence of God. Hannah explained her grief to him, and Eli blessed her. Hannah then left the sanctuary in peace.

In this story Hannah demonstrates private prayer. Hers is the first story of someone coming to a shrine, not for public worship or sacrifice, but simply to speak to God from the heart. She knows how to pour out her troubles to God and remain in God's presence. She is not afraid to explain to the official religious representative what she is doing. He is persuaded by her words and his scolding ends in blessing. When she leaves the sanctuary Hannah's prayer is already answered; God has given peace to her heart.

---

1 Samuel 1:19-28

[19]When they returned Elkanah had intercourse with his wife Hannah, and the LORD remembered her.

[20]She conceived and, at the end of her pregnancy, bore a son whom she named Samuel. "Because I asked the LORD for him." [21]The next time her husband Elkanah was going up with the rest of his household to offer the customary sacrifice to the LORD and to fulfill his vows, [22]Hannah did not go, explaining to her husband, "Once the child is weaned, I will take him to appear before the LORD and leave him there forever." [23]Her husband Elkanah answered her: "Do what you think best; wait until you have weaned him. Only may the LORD fulfill his word!" And so she remained at home and nursed her son until she had weaned him.

[24]Once he was weaned, she brought him up with her, along with a three-year-old bull, an ephah of flour, and a skin of wine, and presented him at the house of the LORD in Shiloh. [25]After they had slaughtered the bull, they brought the child to Eli.

---

1 Samuel 1:19-28 (continued)

[26]Then Hannah spoke up: "Excuse me, my lord! As you live, my lord, I am the woman who stood here near you, praying to the LORD. [27]I prayed for this child, and the LORD granted my request. [28]Now I, in turn, give him to the LORD; as long as he lives, he shall be dedicated to the LORD." Then they worshiped there before the LORD.

God remembers Hannah. Whenever God remembers, something significant happens (cf. Gen 8:1; Exod 2:24). Hannah conceives a son. She names him Samuel and interprets the name to mean "asked of God."[11] As long as Samuel is nursing, Hannah does not go to the sanctuary but remains at home with her child. When he is weaned, she takes Samuel to the sanctuary, along with a generous sacrifice to offer him to God. She not only dedicates him as a perpetual nazirite, she also leaves him in the service of the shrine where the ark is located.

The fact that there is a story of Samuel's infancy indicates that Hannah's son will play a significant role in Israel's salvation history. Just as Moses was instrumental in Israel's move from slavery to freedom, so Samuel is instrumental in the move from tribal leadership to unity under a king. He is the last of the judges; he anoints Israel's first two kings, Saul and David. Both the story of Moses and the story of Samuel begin with courageous and faith-filled women.

Samuel 2:1-10

[1]And Hannah prayed:
"My heart exults in the LORD,
  my horn is exalted by my God.
I have swallowed up my enemies;
  I rejoice in your victory.
[2]There is no Holy One like the LORD;
  there is no Rock like our God.
[3]Speak boastfully no longer,
  Do not let arrogance issue from your mouths.

For an all-knowing God is the LORD,
 a God who weighs actions.
⁴"The bows of the mighty are broken,
 while the tottering gird on strength.
⁵The well-fed hire themselves out for bread,
 while the hungry no longer have to toil.
The barren wife bears seven sons,
 while the mother of many languishes.
⁶"The LORD puts to death and gives life,
 casts down to Sheol and brings up again.
⁷The LORD makes poor and makes rich,
 humbles, and also exalts.
⁸He raises the needy from the dust;
 from the ash heap lifts up the poor,
To seat them with nobles
 and make a glorious throne their heritage.
"For the pillars of the earth are the LORD's,
 and he has set the world upon them.
⁹He guards the footsteps of his faithful ones,
 but the wicked shall perish in the
  darkness;
 for not by strength does one prevail.
¹⁰The LORD's foes shall be shattered;
 the Most High in heaven thunders;
 the LORD judges the ends of the earth.
May he give strength to his king,
 and exalt the horn of his anointed!"

When Hannah dedicates her son to God, she sings a hymn. Thus she joins Miriam and Deborah as the voice of Israel's praise. Many of the phrases of the song echo the psalms. The song's primary theme is God's preference for the poor and powerless. Hannah stands in a long tradition of the *anawim*, the humble people whose total reliance is on God.

God has granted Hannah her heart's desire. There is no god like Israel's God (2:1-2). The Lord humbles those who rely on their own power: the mighty, the well-fed, the fertile wife. The Lord exalts those who know their only hope is in God: the weak, the hungry, the barren wife (2:3-5). All power belongs to God; God uses this power in favor of the lowly (2:6-8). The final stanza of the song restates the theme: It is God who has

power; the power of human beings comes not from their own strength but from God (2:8-10). The final verse, which mentions the king, the anointed (*messiah*), is an anticipation of the work of Hannah's son in making kings.

The song of Hannah is the model for Mary's song (the *Magnificat*) in Luke 1:46-55. Mary, herself one of the *anawim*, is the virgin who bears a son, not through human power but through the power and mercy of God.

---

1 Samuel 2:11-21

¹¹When Elkanah returned home to Ramah, the child remained in the service of the LORD under the priest Eli.

¹²Now the sons of Eli were wicked; they had respect neither for the LORD ¹³nor for the priests' duties toward the people. When someone offered a sacrifice, the priest's servant would come with a three-pronged fork, while the meat was still boiling, ¹⁴and would thrust it into the basin, kettle, caldron, or pot. Whatever the fork brought up, the priest would take for himself. They treated all the Israelites who came to the sanctuary at Shiloh in this way. ¹⁵In fact, even before the fat was burned, the priest's servant would come and say to the one offering the sacrifice, "Give me some meat to roast for the priest. He will not accept boiled meat from you, only raw meat." ¹⁶And if this one protested, "Let the fat be burned first, then take whatever you wish," he would reply, "No, give it to me now, or else I will take it by force." ¹⁷Thus the young men sinned grievously in the presence of the LORD, treating the offerings to the LORD with disdain.

¹⁸Meanwhile the boy Samuel, wearing a linen ephod, was serving in the presence of the LORD. ¹⁹His mother used to make a little garment for him, which she would bring him each time she went up with her husband to offer the customary sacrifice. ²⁰And Eli would bless Elkanah and his wife, as they were leaving for home. He would say, "May the LORD repay you with children from this

continue

Old Testament **canticles** (songs or hymns of praise) are sometimes echoed in the Gospel of Luke as a background for songs found in his story of Jesus. Mary's *Magnificat*, for example, shows great similarities to Hannah's song:

	Hannah's song (1 Sam 2:1-10)		Mary's song (Luke 1:46-55)
2:1	My heart exults in the LORD, my horn is exalted by my God. I have swallowed up my enemies; I rejoice in your victory.	1:46-48	My soul proclaims the greatness of the Lord; my spirit rejoices in God my savior. For he has looked upon his handmaid's lowliness; behold, from now on will all ages call me blessed.
2:2-3	There is no Holy One like the LORD; There is no Rock like our God. Speak boastfully no longer, Do not let arrogance issue from your mouths. For an all-knowing God is the LORD, a God who weighs actions.	1:49-51	The Mighty One has done great things for me, and holy is his name. His mercy is from age to age to those who fear him. He has sown might with his arm, dispersed the arrogant of mind and heart.
2:4	The bows of the mighty are broken, while the tottering gird on strength.	1:52	He has thrown down the rulers from their thrones but lifted up the lowly.
2:5-8	The well-fed hire themselves out for bread, while the hungry no longer have to toil. . . . He raises the needy from the dust; from the ash heap lifts up the poor . . .	1:53	The hungry he has filled with good things; the rich he has sent away empty.
2:9-10	He guards the footsteps of his faithful ones, . . . May he give strength to his king, and exalt the horn of his anointed!	1:54-55	He has helped Israel his servant, remembering his mercy, according to his promise to our fathers, to Abraham and to his descendants forever!

woman for the gift she has made to the LORD!" [21]The LORD favored Hannah so that she conceived and gave birth to three more sons and two daughters, while young Samuel grew up in the service of the LORD.

In the midst of this comparison between Eli's sons and Samuel, Hannah appears for a last time. The regular pilgrimage of Elkanah's family to the sanctuary is mentioned again. Hannah, however, no longer appears as the grieving wife but as the tender mother who brings her little son new clothes every time she comes. Eli remembers Hannah with blessing, and God favors her. She gives birth to five more children, three sons and two daughters. The last verse of Psalm 113 can well be applied to Hannah, for God has given "the childless wife a home, / the joyful mother of children."

CONTINUING THE CONVERSATION

By Jaime L. Waters

Naomi: A Complicated Character

In the book of Ruth, Naomi experiences extreme loss. At the outset, she loses her husband and two sons. Naomi is so grief-stricken that she changes her name to Mara, meaning "bitter," because she feels that God has dealt bitterly with her. Her loss frames the events that unfold in the book, as the loss is emotionally challenging as well as financially and socially damaging. No longer a wife or a mother of living children, Naomi must struggle to survive as a childless widow in a society that frequently affords power and control, especially in public spheres, to men.

An Inspirational Figure

Naomi's actions are decisive for her own survival and the survival of her daughters-in-law, Ruth and Orpah. She initially tells both women who have also lost their husbands that each should return to her "mother's house" (1:8; Hebrew *bet immah*, as in the story of Rebekah in Gen 24:28). While Orpah returns to her family, which would be acceptable and expected, Ruth instead clings to Naomi, affirming her allegiance to Naomi and to the God of Israel in an intense way:

> "Do not press me to go back and
> abandon you!
> Wherever you go I will go,
> wherever you lodge I will lodge.
> Your people shall be my people
> and your God, my God.
> Where you die I will die,
> and there be buried." (Ruth 1:16b-17)

The shared loss helps Naomi and Ruth forge a bond, offering a powerful biblical image of two women in a close relationship with one another. Naomi and Ruth are examples of women's love, friendship, and survival that might inspire readers today.

A Complex Figure

Yet Naomi is a complicated character, and at times her actions could be interpreted in positive or negative ways. On the one hand, Naomi is a survivor, a realist, and a strategist. In Ruth 2, she gives Ruth guidance on how to glean with other women in Boaz's field. She also informs Ruth that Boaz is her relative. In Ruth 3, Naomi states that she wants to gain security for Ruth, so she instructs her on how and where to approach Boaz to initiate and inspire him to act as her redeemer, a legal designation that would offer security and the possibility of having children.

However, these actions could also be read in more nefarious ways. Naomi sends Ruth to glean while she reaps the benefits without doing laborious work (Ruth 2). Because the events on the threshing floor in Ruth 3 can be read with sexual overtones, Naomi might be encouraging Ruth to initiate an illicit and dangerous encounter. In Ruth 4, when Boaz is finally able to redeem Ruth and the property that was in Naomi's family, Ruth has a child who becomes Naomi's child. The action is a part of levirate marriage, which would allow for the child of Ruth and Boaz to be considered a continuation of Naomi's deceased son's line. At the end of the story, Naomi takes the child, cradles and cares for him, and the women in the community proclaim that a son has been born to Naomi (not Ruth).

Overall, the character of Naomi and the relationship between Naomi and Ruth can be very inspirational, yet we must still wrestle with the complex implications of some of the motivations and actions in the text. In doing so, we allow the story to become a more realistic example of the nature of close human relationships, which are often dynamic and multidimensional.

EXPLORING LESSON FIVE

1. How are the causes of migration around the world today similar to the causes in the ancient world (Ruth 1:1, 6)? (See Gen 26:17-22; Exod 2:11-15; 3:7-8; 1 Sam 31:7.)

_____

_____

_____

_____

_____

2. Orpah and Ruth both wrestle with how best to care for Naomi and themselves (Ruth 1:6-18). Has there been any time in your family life or the lives of those close to you when a decision is required about whether to "go back" or "travel on"? (This could be literal or figurative.)

_____

_____

_____

_____

_____

3. What is the practice of gleaning? (See Ruth 2:1-18; see Lev 19:9-10; Deut 24:19-22.) What does this practice tell you about Israel's attitude toward and responsibility for the poor?

_____

_____

_____

_____

4. Re-read Ruth's promise to Naomi in Ruth 1:16-17. How might praying with this passage help you make a deeper commitment not just to God but to God's people?

_____

_____

_____

_____

_____

5. Israel learned lasting lessons of covenant love from Ruth, a foreign woman. What lessons might our church be learning now from those who are different from our regular parish membership?

_____

_____

_____

_____

_____

_____

6. Recall a time when, like Hannah, you pleaded with God to change a situation that seemed hopeless (1 Sam 1:10-17). What difference did your prayer make? Did it change the circumstances? Did it change you?

_____

_____

_____

_____

_____

_____

7. a) What kinds of things happen when the Lord "remembers" (1 Sam 1:19)? (See Gen 8:1-5; 30:22-23; Exod 6:5-6.)

_____

_____

_____

_____

b) What are some biblical truths God is asking *you* to remember? How might these truths change us, if we allow them to? (For examples, see Deut 6:4-6; Isa 43:1-2; Mic 6:8; Matt 5:3-12, 43-48; 6:19-21; John 3:16-17; 1 Cor 13:1-13.)

_____

_____

_____

_____

_____

8. Hannah's song (1 Sam 2:1-10) is a hymn of praise related to her pregnancy and the birth of her child. If you were to write a hymn praising God's recent actions in your life, what would be your theme?

_____

_____

_____

_____

_____

9. Continuing the Conversation: The closing essay presents Naomi as a complex character within the narrative of the book of Ruth. What do you think about this way of interpreting Naomi's character? Does it feel more or less authentic to the biblical text? Does it feel more or less authentic to human experience?

_____

_____

_____

_____

_____

_____

10. a) As you look back on Part One of your study of women in the Old Testament, which woman or story is the most memorable for you and why?

_____

_____

_____

_____

b) What do you most look forward to learning about in Part Two (includes women such as Bathsheba, Jezebel, Eve, Woman Wisdom, Judith, Susanna, and Esther)?

_____

_____

_____

_____

_____

CLOSING PRAYER

Prayer

"[Obed] will restore your life and be the support of your old age, for his mother is the daughter-in-law who loves you. She is worth more to you than seven sons!"   (Ruth 4:15)

God of Naomi and Hannah, God of the hopeful and the hopeless, we praise you for changing desperation into security, and bitterness into joy. Remind us that you are ever watchful and listening, and that when we turn to you, we will be heard and changed. Today, we ask you to accompany those who are fearful, hungry, or anxious, especially . . .

ENDNOTES

1. R. Huniah, "Abraham converted the men and Sarah the women" (Parashah 39:14.1 on Gen 12:5); R. Haninah, "The word is so written as to be read, 'his tent.' Once he had pitched Sarah's tent, he pitched his own" (Parashah 39:15.5 on Gen 12:8). Jacob Neusner, *Genesis Rabbah: The Judaic Commentary to the Book of Genesis. A New American Translation* (Brown Judaic Studies 105; Atlanta: Scholars Press, 1985), 2.74.

2. The story in Genesis 18 is from a tradition sometimes called the Yahwist/J source, so named because it frequently refers to God by the divine name Yahweh (LORD). The story in Genesis 17 is from a tradition often referred to as the Priestly/P source because it reflects priestly concerns, such as an interest in rituals and proper worship. Both the J and P traditions include versions of the birth announcement of Isaac. Because there are scholarly debates about different sources in the Pentateuch, including whether the traditional four source (JEDP) theory is still viable, the J source is now sometimes referred to as the non-P source.

3. Hammurabi, §144–§146. See Victor H. Matthews and Don C. Benjamin, *Old Testament Parallels: Laws and Stories from the Ancient Near East* (New York: Paulist, 2016), 117.

4. Hammurabi §170. See Matthews and Benjamin, 118.

5. Compare Genesis 21:9 where Ishmael is "playing" (*mesaheq*).

6. The translations show the confusion: Septuagint, *astheneis* (weak); Vulgate, *lippis* (inflamed or watery); Douay, bleary-eyed; KJV, tender-eyed; RSV, weak; JB, no sparkle; NEB, dull-eyed; NAB, lovely; NABRE, dull. Some newer translations use "lovely": NJB, NRSV. However, JPS translates "weak," and REB stays with NEB "dull-eyed."

7. Sometimes this word is considered to be *awen*, "trouble" or "sorrow" (Ps 90:10; Hos 9:4). The Greek Septuagint interprets the name *ben-ôni* as "son of my grief."

8. Rebekah was married to Isaac twenty years before the twins were born (Gen 25:20, 26). They grow up and Jacob spends twenty years with Laban (Gen 31:38, 41). At the time of her death the nurse has been in service to Rebekah for at least sixty-five to seventy years.

9. Some scholars posit that Moses' longer song in Exodus 15:1-18 was originally performed by Miriam, especially because women were associated with liturgical song and dance. The longer song may have been attributed to Moses to give it more authority and prestige. The brief mention of Miriam's song in Exodus 15:21 would then be understood as a vestige of a tradition that associates her with the victory song of the exodus.

10. The Hebrew words for woman and man in this passage are not the typical words one might expect, which sheds light on the passage's implications. The word that is translated as woman (*raham*) is related to the word *rehem* which means womb, and in this context, *raham* has more vulgar connotations, such as "a vagina or two for every man." Likewise, the word translated as man (*geber*) is a warrior or strong man, which emphasizes the militaristic context in which overpowering women was considered an acceptable aspect of warfare.

11. The name Samuel actually means "his name is God."

BIBLIOGRAPHY

Bach, Alice, ed. *The Pleasure of Her Text: Feminist Readings of Biblical and Historical Texts*. Philadelphia: Trinity Press International, 1990.

Bellis, Alice O. *Helpmates, Harlots, Heroes: Women's Stories in the Hebrew Bible*. Louisville, KY: Westminster/John Knox, 1994.

Brenner, Athalya. *The Israelite Woman: Social Role and Literary Type in Biblical Narrative*. 2nd ed. London: Bloomsbury, 2015.

Darr, Kathryn Pfisterer. *Far More Precious Than Jewels: Perspectives on Biblical Women*. Gender and the Biblical Tradition. Louisville, KY: Westminster/John Knox, 1991.

Day, Peggy L., ed. *Gender and Difference in Ancient Israel*. Minneapolis: Fortress, 1989.

Gafney, Wilda C. M. *Daughters of Miriam: Women Prophets in Ancient Israel*. Minneapolis: Fortress, 2008.

LaCocque, André. *The Feminine Unconventional: Four Subversive Figures in Israel's Tradition*. Overtures to Biblical Theology. Minneapolis: Fortress, 1990.

McKenna, Megan. *Not Counting Women and Children: Neglected Stories from the Bible*. Maryknoll, NY: Orbis, 1994.

Meyers, Carol. *Rediscovering Eve: Ancient Israelite Women in Context*. Oxford: Oxford University Press, 2013.

Newsom, Carol A., Sharon H. Ringe, and Jacqueline E. Lapsley, eds. *The Women's Bible Commentary*. 3rd ed. Louisville, KY: Westminster/John Knox, 2012.

Nunnally-Cox, J. Ellen. *Foremothers: Women of the Bible*. San Francisco: Harper & Row, 1981.

O'Connor, Kathleen M. *The Wisdom Literature*. Message of Biblical Spirituality 5. Wilmington, DE: Michael Glazier, 1990.

Schüssler-Fiorenza, Elisabeth. *But She Said: Feminist Practices of Biblical Interpretation*. Boston: Beacon Press, 1992.

Sleevi, Mary Lou. *Women of the Word: Art and Story*. Notre Dame, IN: Ave Maria, 1989.

Trible, Phyllis. *God and the Rhetoric of Sexuality*. Overtures to Biblical Theology. Philadelphia: Fortress, 1978.

Trible, Phyllis. *Texts of Terror: Literary-Feminist Readings of Biblical Narratives*. Overtures to Biblical Theology. Minneapolis: Fortress, 2022.

Williams, Delores S. *Sisters in the Wilderness: The Challenge of Womanist God-Talk*. Maryknoll, NY: Orbis Books, 1993.

Winter, Miriam Therese. *WomanWisdom: A Feminist Lectionary and Psalter: Women of the Hebrew Scriptures: Part One*. New York: Crossroad, 1991.

Winter, Miriam Therese. *WomanWitness: A Feminist Lectionary and Psalter: Women of the Hebrew Scriptures: Part Two*. New York: Crossroad, 1991.

PRAYING WITH YOUR GROUP

Because we know that the Bible allows us to hear God's voice, prayer provides the context for our study and sharing. By speaking and listening to God and each other, the discussion often grows to more deeply bond us to one another and to God.

At *the beginning and end of each lesson* simple prayers are provided for individual use, and also may be used within the group setting. Most of the closing prayers provided with each lesson relate directly to a theme from that lesson and encourage you to pray together for people and events in your local community.

Of course, there are many ways to center ourselves in God's presence as we gather together in groups around the word of God. We provide some additional suggestions here knowing you and your group will make prayer a priority as part of your gathering. These are simply alternative ways to pray if your group would like to try something different from those prayers provided in the previous pages.

Conversational Prayer

This form of prayer allows for the group members to pray in their own words in a way that is not intimidating. The group leader begins with Step One, inviting all to focus on the presence of Christ among them. After a few moments of quiet, the group leader invites anyone in the group to voice a prayer or two of thanksgiving; once that is complete, then anyone who has personal intentions may pray in their own words for their needs; finally, the group prays for the needs of others.

A suggested process:
In your own words, speak simple and short prayers to allow time for others to add their voices.

Focus on one "step" at a time, not worrying about praying for everything in your mental list at once.

Step One	Visualize Christ. Welcome him.
	Imagine him present with you in your group.
	Allow time for some silence.
Step Two	Gratitude opens our hearts.
	Use simple words such as, "Thank you, Lord, for . . ."
Step Three	Pray for your own needs knowing that others will pray with you.
	Be specific and honest.
	Use "I" and "me" language.

Step Four   Pray for others by name, with love.
                 You may voice your agreement ("Yes, Lord").
        End with gratitude for sharing concerns.

Praying Like Ignatius

St. Ignatius Loyola, whose life and ministry are the foundation of the Jesuit community, invites us to enter into Scripture texts in order to experience the scenes, especially scenes of the gospels or other narrative parts of Scripture. Simply put, this is a method of creatively imagining the scene, viewing it from the inside, and asking God to meet you there. Most often, this is a personal form of prayer, but in a group setting, some of its elements can be helpful if you allow time for this process.

A suggested process:

- Select a scene from the chapters in the particular lesson.

- Read that scene out loud in the group, followed by some quiet time.

- Ask group members to place themselves in the scene (as a character, or as an onlooker) so that they can imagine the emotions, responses, and thinking that may have taken place. Notice the details and the tone, and imagine the interaction with the Lord that is taking place.

- Share with the group any insights that came to you in this quiet imagining.

- Allow each person in the group to thank God for some insight and to pray about some request that may have surfaced.

Sacred Reading (or Lectio Divina)

This method of prayer invites us to "listen with the ear of the heart" as St. Benedict's rule would say. We listen to the words and the phrasing, asking God to speak to our innermost being. Again, this method of prayer is most often used in an individual setting but may also be used in an adapted way within a group.

A suggested process:

- Select a scene from the chapters in the particular lesson.

- Read the scene out loud in the group, perhaps two times.

- Ask group members to ponder a word or phrase that stands out to them.

- The group members could then simply speak the word or phrase as a kind of litany of what was meaningful for your group.

- Allow time for more silence to ponder the words that were heard, asking God to reveal to you what message you are meant to hear, how God is speaking to you.

- Follow up with spoken intentions at the close of this group time.

REFLECTING ON SCRIPTURE

Reading Scripture is an opportunity not simply to learn new information but to listen to God who loves you. Pray that the same Holy Spirit who guided the formation of Scripture will inspire you to correctly understand what you read, and empower you to make what you read a part of your life.

The inspired word of God contains layers of meaning. As you make your way through passages of Scripture, whether studying a book of the Bible or focusing on a biblical theme, you may find it helpful to ask yourself these four questions:

What does the Scripture passage say?
Read the passage slowly and reflectively. Become familiar with it. If the passage you are reading is a narrative, carefully observe the characters and the plot. Use your imagination to picture the scene or enter into it.

What does the Scripture passage mean?
Read the footnotes in your Bible and the commentary provided to help you understand what the sacred writers intended and what God wants to communicate by means of their words.

What does the Scripture passage mean to me?
Meditate on the passage. God's word is living and powerful. What is God saying to you? How does the Scripture passage apply to your life today?

What am I going to do about it?
Try to discover how God may be challenging you in this passage. An encounter with God contains a challenge to know God's will and follow it more closely in daily life. Ask the Holy Spirit to inspire not only your mind but your life with this living word.